# LEADERSHIP AND TRAINING FOR THE FIGHT

## A FEW THOUGHTS ON LEADERSHIP AND TRAINING FROM A FORMER SPECIAL OPERATIONS SOLDIER

## MSG PAUL R. HOWE
## U.S. ARMY RETIRED

authorHOUSE™

1663 LIBERTY DRIVE, SUITE 200
BLOOMINGTON, INDIANA 47403
(800) 839-8640
WWW.AUTHORHOUSE.COM

First published by AuthorHouse 06/22/06

ISBN: 1-4208-8951-6 (e)
ISBN: 1-4208-8950-8 (sc)

Library of Congress Control Number: 2005908858

Printed in the United States of America
Bloomington, Indiana

This book is printed on acid-free paper.

# DEDICATION

I would like to dedicate this book to the following:
- My Wife
- The Men and Women who serve in our Armed Forces
- The Law Enforcement Community

**My Wife** has helped me carry my rucksack through life with unwavering support and dedication. Without her consummate stability, I could not have made this journey with the success I have found.

**The Men and Women who serve in our Armed Forces.** The Army provided me a home where I could learn and grow for a great deal of my life. It's mediocrity pushed me to improve and Special Ops gave me a home to grow. Special thanks go to the Non-Commissioned Officers (NCO's) who set the example and taught me to push farther and faster with greater precision, not because it was required, but because it was the right thing to do. Also thanks for the confirmation in doing what is right versus what is popular.

**The Law Enforcement Community** is the glue that holds our country together. Generally underpaid, under trained and overworked, they continue to protect and serve for the right reasons.

# NOTE TO READER

Out of courtesy to my former unit and their sensitive nature, many of my descriptions are referred to as "Special Operations." I have attempted to "sanitize" this work as much as possible. Having said this, all incidents are as accurate as my memory can recall. Also remember that my perception is based on my cumulative experiences in the military and law enforcement community. My view may vary from others and my expectations of an individual or unit may weigh in on this. A former commander often said, "to whom much is given, much is expected."

I have grown older and wiser over the years, gaining a bit more insight and understanding into life. With that said, I try not to judge soldiers on an individual action, but take a comprehensive look at their training, leadership and then individual heart.

Thanks for your understanding.

# FINAL EDITION

As I stated in the first edition, my goal with this project was to publish it in a timely manner (sometime before I die) so that others may learn from it and stay alive because of it. I have allowed a few professionals that I have work with to help clean up spelling and grammar errors. With that, I deliberately have not let a college professor or professional proofreader edit this project. My reasons are simple. I believe this would dilute the work and would not give an accurate portrayal of who I am, how I speak and what I intended to say.

Since the initial publication of this work, I have received numerous reviews and most of them were positive. Readers have urged me to keep the content as is. They felt that it lends itself to the credibility of the project. Combat is not polished, but sometimes brutal, disjointed and simply rough around the edges. With that, this will be the final corrected version of this work as I wish to put it to bed and move on to other writing projects.

When reading, try not to trip over dollar bills to pick up pennies. Look at the concepts and ideas and see if you can apply them in your trials. My target audience is the man or woman in the arena. I hope the lessons I learned help them on their future missions to come home and bring those around them back alive.

Thank you for your comments, patience and understanding,
Paul Howe

# FORWARD

After giving it much thought (and with a little practical experience) I have come to the conclusion that our society, or way of life, will not come to an end because of a natural disaster or through a superior enemy, but rather through a lack of leadership and initiative on our part. Leadership is what has made our country and what will "break" our country. Leadership permeates all folds of military and law enforcement tactical training and operations. Generally, success or failure of the mission can be tracked down to a leadership void in the selection or training of the personnel at the individual, team or organizational level of the tactical element. Leadership is not rocket science. Positive leadership requires only that the leader follow simple and common sense rules and practices to ensure success or failure of an assigned mission.

I have been prodded over the years by friends, students and colleagues to put my thoughts and experiences on paper in the form of a book. I hesitated initially for security reasons, but I also felt that Mark Bowden did an exceptional job of tying together all the individual and leadership actions in his book, "Black Hawk Down." These were actions that military leaders at the time attempted to sweep under the carpet due to the political fallout. Also, I hesitated because of self-doubt in my writing ability and my self-confidence in putting this work together in a comprehensive and easy to understand package, that could be used as a reference for future generations. I eventually gave in and decided to attack this matter head on. Further, I believe at the age of 45, I feel I now have enough experience and understanding to write in a clear and focused manner. Remembering the words of an old friend and former Secret Service Agent, Carl Kovalchik who said, "I am not trying to learn new stuff, I am just trying to remember what I have." With that,

I want to try and capture the focus and aggression I had as a younger man and not try to re-interpret it as a "kinder-gentler" middle aged FAG (Former Action Guy).

I knew that when I started this project it would prove to be a continual work in progress, as is life. I will reference sources in this work that I deem accurate, viable and in the end, those that inspired and helped me in my learning process and survival. I will use a great deal of my life experiences that I can recall, and as important, my mindset at the time of the learning experience or incident that helped me survive it. I have found that your mindset plays a key point in action, interaction, understanding and development. As I get older, I find I gain a clarity of thought and the patience to put on paper, what escaped me as a younger man, who's testosterone and excess energy tended to get in the way of a clear communication process.

Why write on leadership? Too many times in our lives we find ourselves saddled with ticket punching ladder climbers and those who seek the role of leader for the wrong reasons.

"Those who seek leadership most are seldom suited for it."

Attributed to an unnamed Confederate officer

Whether political or military, many times we find the system skewed with leaders who wish to guide men, but have cheated in their own life and experiences. There are some who are self-serving cowards that climbed over good people to attain their goals. Poor leadership in the business world will cost you time and money. In the military and law enforcement world, it will cost the lives of our mothers, fathers, sons and daughters.

This book is not based on leadership theory, but a practiced system used and tested under the worse case scenario, combat. In my eyes, the validation of a leadership system culminated on 3-4 October 1993 in a one-sided battle in Mogadishu, Somalia. There I saw leadership at the individual, team and organizational level both excel and fail. Within these pages I hope to enlighten you as to the techniques that succeeded and those that fell short and why. I will do my best to show you the path needed to achieve success in personal combat and on the battlefield as a unit. There are many more battles to be fought and won to ensure our survival and way of life.

# TABLE OF CONTENTS

# CHAPTER ONE

# ACCELERATING THE LOOP

*"The speed must come from a deep intuitive understanding of one's relation to the rapidly changing environment"*

Robert Coram from "Boyd: The Fighter Pilot Who Changed The Art of War."

- BOYD'S THEORY AND INDIVIDUAL COMBAT
- INSIDE YOUR ENEMY'S MIND
- ESTABLISHING A REFERENCE POINT IN YOUR MIND
- OBSERVE
- ORIENT
- DECIDE
- ACT
- SOME THOUGHTS ON INDIVIDUAL COMBAT AND TRAINING

## NEAR MISSES

It was the dead of night and we were flying in low level, trying to avoid TV and radio antennas that could be a show stopper should we collide with one. I was sitting to the rear of the pod and I got the one-minute index finger signal from the pilot. I started looking ahead at the buildings and I was trying to pinpoint our target. It was a multi-story walled compound that held a potential hiding place for our top personality. Flying a U.N. flag, this target was reputed to be dirty.

In the same compound was an adjacent multi-story building that was a secondary target and potential hiding place for our target. Teams were assigned to enter and clear this target as well as our primary target building. I was still trying to pinpoint our building, which had a distinctive roof design and a certain type of antenna. I was scanning hard on our final approach and things did not look right. Instead of depositing our entire force on one building, the pilots let the force off on three separate buildings. I saw a bird to our rear let off a team on a building 40-50 meters to our rear, inside another walled compound. I knew this could be dangerous because our chain of command had briefed us that security forces were present on buildings either side of our target building.

I jumped off my pod, hitting the ground and going to a knee. We had a three foot parapet on the top of our building, which protected us from hostile fire. At the base of the inner parapet were floodlights that were shinning out through the slits in the parapet wall. I tried taking the light out with a butt stroke from my weapon stock, but the butt of my "plastic" stock just bounced off. I found a piece of broken concrete within arms reach and gave it a good smash and the light went out.

I started scanning to our rear and saw that the team behind us was on top of their building and appeared to be shooting out their floodlights. I could see the silhouette of an operator, back lit from one of the lights. The team was indeed on top of the roof, shooting out their lights with their car-15's. All of a sudden, someone fired two shots next to my head, the tracers screaming past the team member on top of the building to our rear. I struck the shooter (my partner) in the helmet with a backhanded closed fist and shouted "cease fire," those are friendlies. Evidently he had not been scanning deep enough with his Night Vision Goggles (NVG's) and not seen the bird let one of our teams on the roof to our rear.

The two rounds fired were tracer and I could not see if they connected with one of the team members because as they streaked by, he dropped down so fast, it looked like he was hit. The rounds kept going and I could see an inbound helo jerk hard to avoid the rounds. My heart sank at the thought of a friendly fire casualty. I could understand why my partner shot, he heard and saw gunfire, saw the silhouette with a gun and was briefed that it was a hostile building. I only hoped that he had missed, but this would create another dilemma for me as a team leader, the fact that he did miss.

I knew that we were probably on the wrong building, but did not want to stay on top and become a bullet magnet or pinned down from the ground. I led the team down a rickety metal spiral staircase on the outside of the building. The team started taking names and kicking ass. People had been sleeping in the courtyard and were coming out of the woodwork, waking up and looking at us through their squinting eyes. As I ran into one guy and he spun off me. I turned around and white lighted him with my gun light. When the light hit him, he acted as if I shot him. He put his hands up in front of his face and he crumbled backward to the ground.

Team members were starting to flex-tie individuals and I was trying to link-up with another team leader to find out where the target building was in relationship to our positions. I found another team leader from another building and asked him if any of his guys were hit, still worrying about the two tracer rounds. He said his guys were good to go.

Just then, our bird reappeared and hovered above our roof. Outstanding. The pilots had come back to get us and re-insert us on the right roof. I gathered the team and we climbed the shaky staircase one final time. I was just hoping that it would support our weight one more time. We got to the roof, took or our seats on the bird and took off for the right target building. A couple of minutes later, we got to the right target and I could see several teams already on the roof.

To my amazement, they had not blown the roof door or penetrated the building. It seems the assault force was spread over several buildings and everyone got there late. The door was blown and we started clearing. We cleared the third and then second floor and conducted a link-up with a team working its way up from the bottom. We went back to the roof and found an outside second floor door that was not open and we threw a fast rope over the edge and had one guy body wrap it while we slid down to the next landing. We just wanted to ensure that we did not miss anything.

Upon securing the building, we gathered up our package and cleared the courtyard buildings and vehicles, which was our secondary mission. It was clear and we conducted a link-up with our perimeter teams at the front gate. We consolidated our assault force and moved about a block on foot to a hasty helicopter-landing zone in a walled courtyard.

Upon arrival, I started asking questions as to whether or not the area had been cleared. The problem was that the landing area had 10-15 rooms facing the bird from an adjacent building and had not yet been cleared. The team and I started clearing the rooms to ensure our incoming bird would be safe. Just as I thought, there were families in some of these rooms that were frightened and huddled in corners. We conducted a hasty search for weapons and then motioned for them to stay put. The last thing you want is a gunfight in close quarters with a helicopter in the middle of it, with guns pointing in all directions and the possibility of civilians running into the action or a tail rotor.

## AFTER ACTION COMMENTS

### Sustain:

- Aggressiveness
- Follow through on mission

### Improve:

- Friendly fire briefings and Rules of Engagement. Look harder and be sure of your target
- Communicate faster to team members when under NVG's as you have tunnel vision and might not be seeing the same things
- Counsel subordinate on shooting? Counsel subordinate on missing?

# BOYD'S THEORY AND INDIVIDUAL COMBAT

Colonel John Boyd has been described as one of the principle military geniuses of the 20<sup>th</sup> century and few know his name or accomplishments. Nicknamed "40-Second" Boyd, because it was his standing invitation to pilots that from a position of disadvantage, he would turn the dogfight around and be on his opponents tail within 40 seconds. The rumor is that he never lost. More important than the challenge, was Boyd's ability to articulate his winning strategy and teach it to others.

Boyd's OODA (Observe, Orient, Decide, Act) loop or theory has been explained in several different fashions and interpreted by each audience in a different way. On paper the loop takes a more linear approach consisting of Observe > Orient > Decide > Act. A simplistic view of the cycle or loop would be that you "Observe" the enemy and their actions. Next you would "Orient" yourself or force into a more favorable position. You would then "Decide" on your course of action. Finally, you would take "Action." According to Robert Coram, the author of "Boyd: The Fighter Pilot Who Changed The Art of War," Boyd's intent was not a speedy mechanical solution, but rather to implement the cycle in a way to get inside your opponent's mind and to disrupt his decision making cycle by ensuring that they are dealing with outdated or irrelevant information which does not allow them to make a decision or to function.

As stated in the beginning, Boyd's successful use of the loop involved compressing time (the loop) in a faster manner than your opponent. He said, "The speed must come from a deep intuitive understanding of one's relationship to the rapidly changing environment." In effect, the one who learns to move through the loop faster than their opponent, will generally win. There are some circumstances where this may not apply, but generally it will ensure your success. A case cited by Coram is that of General Patton and WWII tactics and feats. Instead of giving specific mission orders to seize a specific spot of ground, it was suggested that a broader mission statement of "intent" be used. This intent would enable forces on the ground to use their own initiative and exploit weaknesses as they saw fit. This "empowerment" aimed at the lower levels of leadership is extremely successful. The use of this technique also provides more efficient strides and gains in battle. Instead of throwing all assets or forces at a particular strongpoint, an "empowerment or trust" was pushed to maneuver elements allowing them to "use their heads" and select the path that would enable them to accomplish the mission with the greatest chance of survival. What a concept! This in itself would create a force for planning, initiative and aggressiveness, which would have a direct impact on survival. This, in my eyes, would bring critically needed motivation and thought out and into most combat scenarios. In Patton's case, he would attack through the initial layers of the enemies defense, ignoring his flanks, creating chaos not only there and throughout the enemies forces, both with the troops on the line, but also with the support troops. It is the above case that is in the minds of the support troops. They are greatly effected by the chaos and the fear of the unknown who we can mentally catch and exploit in the OODA Loop.

## INSIDE YOUR ENEMY'S MIND

> Coram reports Boyd stated, "Machines don't fight wars,
> terrain doesn't fight wars. You must get into the minds
> of humans. That's where the battles are won."

This may seem a bit deep, but it is actually pretty simple. Once you learn to use the loop, you can employ simple and effective tactics that will "shock and disorient" your opponent long enough for you to seize the initiative, better position yourselves for the act phase, eliminate (kill) them from the loop and then find another victim to apply your loop to. This concept applies to the strategic level, the battlefield, the team and individual levels of combat.

To help your understanding, let's apply this concept to an individual "running and gunning" on an assault, where your force is tasked to push through an enemy fortification. In this case, the enemy is on the defense and they have prepared a suitable response plan to repel any attack. Their first line of defense is to fire mortars or artillery at the attacking force. The next line of defense is for individual soldiers to directly fire their rifles and Rocket Propelled Grenades (RPG'S) at the attackers. Once the attackers get into hand grenade range (35 meters) they will throw these killer eggs in your direction, all while still firing their primary weapons. Once you get close, the enemy plans to fall back to alternate positions and continue to engage you.

The enemy intends to do all this in an orderly process, so this is where we bring chaos and disorder to their plan. First, we drop cluster bombs on their positions from aircraft. Next we call in some artillery shells, some that air burst and some that go deep in the ground and then explode, causing large craters, moving tons of earth in the span of a second. We then fire white phosphorus rounds, which burns everything that it comes into contact with to prevent the enemy from observing our approach. By this time, all but hardened enemy soldiers are frightened animals. Their artillery is neutralized. The landscape does not look the same as it did when they went into their holes. The enemy has limited visibility as the area is on fire and smoking. They cannot see the attackers, but are taking effective fire from them. A bleak picture indeed.

Now picture this, the entire attacking force has bypassed you, thinking you are not significant and they are pushing deep into your rear areas. In effect, you are surrounded. Think about your mindset now. Dead and wounded are strewn about the rubbled landscape. Occasional mortar rounds are still exploding, letting you know that someone is still thinking of you and they still have you under their guns. More armored vehicles are passing by, out of the reach of your guns. A majority of regular soldiers would probably think about giving in.

At the individual level, it gets even more intense. You hear the sound of explosions getting closer. As you poke your head around a corner for a look, the concrete explodes in your eyes where the bullets strike the wall, narrowly missing your head. The last glimpse you saw as you fall backward a step and try and shake it off was that of several shapes closing in on you. You learned your lesson about sticking your head out around corners. You regain your composure and prepare to angle your weapon around the corner and give a burst of automatic fire to give the attackers something to think about. Yeah, you think to yourself, I'm doing good. Just then, you notice a small round and green object lumber past the corner about three feet from you. Your eyes focus on it and you realize it is a fragmentation grenade and then it explodes. You feel the steel pushing through parts of your body and you fall backward from the blast. You try to stand, but for some reason, your upper leg seems to push past your lower leg and touch the ground. You try to take a breath and you realize that it is like trying to breath through a sopping wet handkerchief. You then realize the reason for this is that a great deal of your lungs are sticking to the wall behind you. As you gurgle for air and as your vision dims, the last picture your mind snaps is that of an American flash suppressor spitting fire in your face.

Too late, someone has moved through the loop faster and more efficiently than you. So, how do we make this happen and end up on the right end of the flash suppressor? We learn to move through the loop faster, more efficiently and with more focus than our opponent. How can this be accomplished? By breaking down the entire process into simple and decisive actions. Will technology give us an edge? You bet. At times technology will aid in all portions of the loop. Within the next few sections, I will give you my view as how to best accelerate the loop at the individual, team and organizational level, as well as giving you a few simple techniques that will help you to accelerate your personal, team and organizational journey through the loop.

# OBSERVE

## Individual Level

The first step in accelerating the loop at the individual level is to teach the person to observe, or "become conscious of" their surroundings. I will use an urban environment as an example. Subconsciously, after years of training and combat, I learned "where to look" and not waste valuable time scanning the entire area. Instead of looking at everything in the environment, walls, trees, cars, roofs, etc., I focused on where a person could shoot at you from. If you tried to look at everything, *you are already getting behind in the loop* because you are overloading your brain with useless information and images. It is not a blank wall, or on the ground in front of you where an enemy gunman is going to shoot from, but rather that doorway on the right, the wall to your center or the window to the left. Knowing this, you can focus on the battlefield and narrow your scanning to relevant information. You might have caught movement or fire from a window and suppressed it. The reason for catching movement in the window is that it has a higher priority in your scanning sequence than other areas and you may scan it twice as much as lower threat areas.

### Team Level

The same process can be used for team movement, but your point or lead person is focused on the front, while other members are going to be watching their "sectors (assigned areas)," such as an alley to the left or right. These areas might be constantly changing and shifting. When looking at the alley, team members should be looking at the leading edges of buildings for signs of people. Muzzle flashes, dust clouds and shadows are indicators of threats. By looking at the edges and not the center of the alley, team members are picking up threats faster than going from the blank center of a street to a wall.

### Organizational Level

Simply by expanding the above philosophy that I have described, your organizational element will reap the benefits of the individual and team observations. Your empowered elements will see further and faster than their adversaries and report this information back or take action on it, depending upon what you instructed them to do in their mission orders

### Observation Training

Today's technology and optics can greatly enhance this portion of the loop and can cut your visual pick up time for threats and/or targets. At the individual level, a variable scope on a soldier's rifle in an urban or open environment may aid the speed of observation. I recommend that optics be run on the lowest power because an immediate threat may present itself and take up the entire field of view. Use your normal scanning and vision to alert you to danger areas and then use the "cam" on your scope to increase the magnification or view to more easily see your area or point in question. I remember one action when the bad guys knew our rules of engagement. They knew that if we could not see a weapon, we could not shoot. They tried using it against us by sawing off their AK-47's and wrapping them in a sheet or towel. An unaided eye at one to two blocks away made it almost impossible to see a weapon. However, with a small bit of magnification, it became easy to see the outline of a front sight post, the pistol grip or an entire weapon. This visual allowed you to comply with the rules of engagement and service those threats. I returned from this trip and promptly bought a 1.5 x 4.5 compact scope for just this reason. The same theory goes for our long range and standoff weapons, including tanks and helicopters. The further out we can see, the further out we can engage. This will generally speed your way through the loop and ultimately impact on the cumulative tactical time.

How can we improve our observation and scanning sequence at the individual level? Simple, develop scanning exercises that teach individuals to see fast. I routinely ask students if they shoot first or see first. The answer is obvious. They must see first, before they can shoot. In one portion of the scanning sequence, I train students to discriminate. In the old days when I was first assigned to Special Ops, they taught us to look at the hands first. As emphasis was placed on our shooting skills and speed, our shooting developed faster than our scanning skills. As a result, discrimination suffered and friendly fire accidents increased. Individuals were looking at the hands, bringing their weapons to center mass of their target, squeezing one to two rounds off and their brain would catch up and say, "Uh-oh, " that is a friendly officer. I have witnessed this with paintball, simunitions, live fire exercises, and in combat. Consequently, I have changed my scanning process to look at the whole person first, see who it is and then collapse to the hands.

The drill I use to enhance an officers scanning process is a simple one. I have 50 pre-made targets that I set up in a classroom size room. Twenty five are set up in depth on one side and 25 are on the other. On the command to enter, two students enter and go to their sector and must scan the 25 targets for the one with the gun. When all is said and done, each target must be scanned three times each. First, whole person and then you collapse to right/left or left/right hand. With that simple drill on one side only, 75 scans need to be made. I video students' first attempts at the drill, their entry and scanning sequence. Usually the same problems are present, weapons too high in the visual plane, scanning too fast, not scanning far enough, etc. I teach the students to develop a systematic scanning sequence that goes from hard points in the room, points that don't change from room to room and push them to do the whole person and hands. As they hit the room several more times, they practice their system and their speed increases.

Another problem that comes into play is the visual overload upon entering the room. I do not allow them to see the room prior to entry. Upon entry, they are visually overwhelmed and do not resort to the scanning system that I teach in class. Routinely they will be standing right next to the threat target and not even see it, even after they give an "all clear" that the room is free from threat targets. I intentionally attempt to visually overwhelm them and force them to consciously focus their scanning on pertinent information that you would find on the battlefield or in a raid type scenario. This drill has humbled many a seasoned officer. In addition, it is inexpensive to set-up and can be practiced without firing a shot. This same drill can be performed with a team and taken to the next level by including video graphics. As in real life, those practicing most video games know where the threat is going to expose itself from and we in turn set ourselves up in the most advantageous spot to engage it. This is where the "Orient" step comes into play, allowing students to see and place themselves in a tactically advantageous position.

## ORIENT

The individual orient phase can be thought of as "posturing" or preemptively assuming a tactically superior position. In the observation phase, you have already observed and are aware of the threat areas facing you. You now need to adjust your individual position and maneuver to an offensively superior position. Note I did not say defensive, I said offensive. You must posture yourself in such a way as to maintain maximum cover and aggressively maneuver on the threat.

Take for example the street movement described in the earlier section. Individuals should move in such a way as to visually obscure their movement from the enemy while keeping them in constant view. Gunfights are nothing more that successfully using geometric angles to protect yourself as much of the time as possible. During movement, try and expose as little of your body as possible for the shortest time possible and make yourself a small/hard target. In other words, make the bad guy expose more of themselves to you, in their effort to put you under effective fire. This increases your chances of hitting them sooner and faster. Use natural and manmade objects as "cover" to make these movements. Put trees, walls, cars, etc., between you and your objective in order to get closer, thereby denying them the physical and mental advantage.

## Team

At the team level do the same, but lead the team on the most covered and concealed route to the enemy. To give you an added advantage, your team should have a decisive reaction drill to contact and automatically deploy when taking fire. This should be a type of non-verbal communication. Such non-verbal communication works as follows: If team members see or hear you shoot, that is a non-verbal form of communication and they know to automatically execute the planned drill. We thereby eliminate the verbal command from the process, further expediting our ride through the loop. This can take the form of an Immediate Action Drill (IAD) such as being fired upon when moving to the front door of your planned target. We plan on this because we have worked in this environment and we know that once the first round is fired, you can't hear (auditory exclusion) and the visual becomes your primary source of information.

### *Organization*

The organization is an extension of the team and all the same rules apply. Individual teams making up the organization should be applying all the same tactics and techniques in their individual battles or firefights to ensure their desired outcome.

## Training for the Orientation Phase

Training at the individual level is relatively simple, reinforcing all the basic soldier or police officer skills dealing with the use of cover and concealment. Both the soldier and the officer should understand cover and concealment and when to use each. Cover is an object, manmade or natural, that will protect the soldier from fire, such as a concrete walls or a dirt berm. Cover will stop bullets and shrapnel. Concealment is simply a visual barrier that stops an opponent from seeing you, but it will not stop bullets. Concealment might consist of hedges or shrubs around a house. It is critical to ensure that the individual understands what cover is and how to use it. They should constantly put it between the enemy and themselves to greatly enhance the chances of survival.

Training the team for this phase is a bit more complicated. The team must learn the safety aspects of fire and maneuver, weapon handling and, when to shoot, etc. Team members must continually scan for cover, both individually and as a team. A team who decides to hide behind one tree, makes it easy for the enemy to put effective fire on them, especially when you are in a line of ducks. Individuals need to look in the "zone" or immediate area for suitable cover. Once contact has been initiated and the team is taking fire, the teams needs to have a simple and effective battle drill that can be initiated in the event of non-verbal communication (gunfire).

Further, these drills need to be in sections or modules so they can be easily remembered. For example, as previously described, a team should have a contact drill when moving to a door or breach point on a potential target. The drill should be simple, generally the same each time and easy to execute. By keeping it simple, your mind can catalog it and prioritize it every time you come into a high risk situation. Depending on your career field, it might be a routine occurrence. In simple terms, how many times do either military or police have to move to the front door of a residence or compound. You need to develop a simple method for this and do it all the time so you will become extremely good at it. Doing it over and over will reinforce your tactic and make you extremely proficient at it. To reiterate, look at one phase of the assault, movement to the breach point. This action must be accomplished on every target of every mission. It applies to hostage rescue, high-risk warrants, search warrants and barricaded persons. Developing and implementing one technique that will work for all missions is helping your soldiers or officers at ground level by requiring them to have fewer and simpler drills which will allow them to react more efficiently in a high stress situation. They will have less mental clutter to distract them.

Validating your drill should be a prime concern and focus. How do we do this? As described before, live role players, scripted scenarios, and video are the key. Develop five worse case core scenarios that are likely to happen and develop tactics to solve these problems. These tactics should ensure the maximum safety and survival of your forces while putting effective and decisive fire on the enemy. Also, reviewing worse case scenarios ensures one of two things are likely to happen. If you don't encounter the worse case scenario in training, it may hit you in combat. If you are lucky and don't plan for this worse case scenario in your first training cycle, you will probably find it later and have to do double work and adjust the current training or relearn another drill to solve this new problem. Ensure that you use video to record the actions and look at it from all angles. I like to video from above, so I can see how people move and where their weapons are pointing. Also, by using brightly colored paintballs, you can actually see how the fire is distributed on the battlefield. This can also be done with tracers in a day or night exercise to see how well your men are hitting their targets or how effectively the fires are massed against your enemy. If feasible, allow all your personnel to watch the video to gain a better understanding of what the big picture is and their part of it. As is elsewhere in life, knowledge is power.

# DECIDE

### Individual Decisions

The individual decision making process should be simple and efficient. The most efficient way to deal with this issue is to simplify and interpret the Rules of Engagement (ROE). ROE should be designed for the lowest member of the element to understand and react to a threat in an efficient manner. ROE in the military are generally written by Staff Judge Advocate (JAG) personnel or lawyers by another name. Since lawyers are generally too educated to produce a simplified ROE sheet, some ROE sheets can run a page long. A page of writing in the mind of a private is too much information. The private, sometimes carrying a crew-served weapon such as a light machine gun, can do a lot of damage under the right conditions. Conversely, a private failing to shoot at the right time can enable an enemy to gain the offensive and you to lose the window of opportunity to inflict maximum casualties.

This window of opportunity I discussed may be hampered when a private is confused by a complex ROE. The private should have a streamlined ROE than enables him to make a split second decision that will weigh in his favor. Bad guys do not have a death wish; however, most wish to survive the confrontations, as we would. Having said this, they may approach you and not see you until you open fire on them. Either you hit them or you don't, but if you don't, they may scurry for cover, drop their weapon and jump outside your ROE box. They may decide that hauling ass away from the engagement is their best chance of survival. "Technically" a soldier cannot shoot them when they depart, unless they are carrying a weapon. These combatants could be running to get another weapon, but you have to ensure that you have a supportive chain of command, should you decide to shoot. Should the soldier be uncertain of the ROE and the bad guy spots our soldier first, he may elect to do the same thing and run from the area. The private with his big gun needs to understand when he can shoot and when he cannot and make best use of his weapon system. A team leader may not be present when someone comes into your field of view and it may be solely up to you whether you shoot or not. A team leader may be five feet from you and he does not have your visual angle and may fail to see the threat. Consequently, an individual needs to know when they can pull the trigger and when they cannot.

How do we simplify this process at the individual level? Easy. We take the same basic concept that we use for self-defense in the United States and we transfer it overseas. If you feel your life or the life of another is in imminent danger of death or great bodily harm, you can use deadly force to protect yourself or others. It is true that team leaders and sergeants may have to use examples to illustrate this concept to their young men or women. In the end, the decision making process should be simple. It should take longer to switch a weapon safety to fire and pull a trigger, than to make a decision whether to shoot or not to shoot.

These decisions can be complicated today by the enemy's attempt to confuse us by wearing civilian clothes in combat. Of course I prefer it as the bright colors provide a better background to your front sight. Joking aside, in combat a threat is a threat, whether in civilian clothes or not. A rocket propelled grenade and launcher is not some new fashion statement, but rather a deadly threat. The same thought process can be said for non combatants rushing to a gunfight. They are not coming for some social purpose, but rather to aid the enemy and they should be considered a threat.  I have witnessed them bringing ammunition to enemy positions, spot and direct fire for enemy gunners and haul enemy wounded away.  In all these cases, under proper ROE, they have lost their "civilian" status and are actively aiding the enemy.  Further, if they are not running away from the battle, they are keeping bad company.  Once again, these individuals have forsaken their civilian status and should be considered a combatant.  If you catch someone looking around a corner without a weapon and they see you, they should run in the opposite direction.  If they fail to run and look again, they are spotting for an enemy soldier and they are plotting against you.  The next time they look, they should see your front sight post and your right eye staring at them, then a flash from the end of your barrel.

The goal now should be to condition our soldiers to think the same way and break them out of the "uniformed military" thought process. We have grown up preaching that our enemies will be in uniforms and when we don't see these uniforms, our forces hesitate in firing.  Or once they do fire, they have remorse and second thoughts that they have done something bad.  This needs to be addressed before the battle and the leadership needs to praise and reinforce their belief that the individuals did the right thing.

### Team Decisions

Team decisions should not vary from the individual ones, but rather team actions should be enhanced by the individuals quick thinking and actions.  The faster the individual reacts to a situation, the faster the team will maneuver to back them up and provide additional fire support. Again, to start the process rolling, it takes the individual to be alert and decisive.  Further, decisiveness at the individual level should be rewarded and reinforced, not punished.

### Organizational Decisions

As with the team process of decision making, the organization will be able to react or respond faster if the individuals and teams make faster assessments and decisions.  The organization may have other plans at the time and may be waiting for the precise moment to prepare a decisive strike.  For example, you may "bait" the enemy in with a feint of sorts and project an illusion of weakness where you then liberally apply large doses of bombs, artillery and direct fire to his massed forces.

This was an unintended result of actions in Somalia in 1993. When the Somali National Alliance (SNA-Bad Guys) thought that the Task Force Ranger was pinned down, they began gathering their forces from all over the city in waves to come in and assault the defensive perimeter. As they would come down the streets in groups of 40-50 people, little bird gun ships would fly in between buildings and chew them up with their mini-guns. You would have thought that the Somali's learning curve would have gone up. It did not and they did it again and again. They unintentionally threw their people into a meat grinder and allowed the pilots to keep their guns warm. Never before could we get all their forces in one place to engage them in such an efficient manner. The pilots took advantage of this and quickly attrited the enemies fighting force.

## Teaching Decision Making

Teaching decision making is a process that has improved over the years by better technology and by the instruction of theory. Over 25 years ago, law enforcement used wax bullets on a white wall or background while a scenario was projected. We have similar, though better, technology today in the form of visual interactive simulators and live role players. Interactive simulations can be played with lasers and provide you with both the decision making process and the requirement to make accurate shots to stop your opponent. Simunitions and live role players can add a bit more stress with a true to life picture and scenario of a problem. The scenario can be replayed or an element added or deleted at a moments notice.

Simulations should not be limited to the individual level, but must also be required of the command personnel. If we are all affected by the same decision making process during a high stress situation, why not require a leader who makes all encompassing life and death decisions affecting an entire force to also rehearse or practice these decisions? Sadly, there is no requirement for such leadership training. Only extraordinary leaders take the initiative and seek out this training. Generally, most of today's officers feel that they don't need the training or it is too easy. Yet these are the same officers who are overwhelmed in the stress of combat while trying to process all the incoming information under chaotic conditions. Today's combat is fast, intense and lethal requiring leaders to make positive and rapid decisions faster than ever before. The training discussed in this section should be a mandatory requirement for leadership.

# ACT

### Individual

The "Act" phase is where I place most of my emphasis. The most fundamental act is pulling a trigger. As Special Operations soldiers, we spent a majority of our time on the range, perfecting our skills. This was a luxury we took full advantage of. The first three steps in the loop are important in order to reach the "Act" stage. Using the "Act" of making a surgical shot at say seven yards with a pistol, I will attempt to put this step in the loop in relation to the other steps. I train to make my first shot from a high ready position, a position where the handgun is close into the body, muzzle slightly up and generally following my eyes as they scan. As I observe a potential target, I have already oriented my body to the act and I determine that a target is bad, I commit or act, firing the shot. The act itself is pushing the weapon out, taking the slack out of the trigger at the same time, catching the front sight as it comes up on target and dropping it into my rear sight, breaking the shot as this happens. I practice to do all this in one second or less and hit a six inch by twelve inch kill zone resembling a spinal column on a target at seven yards. I have refined my "act" phase to accomplishing the task in less than one second, routinely attaining the .90 second mark.

How do you get there? Repetition and muscle memory. Top shooters in life "dry practice" 70 percent to 30 percent live fire. In other words, for every time you fire live rounds, you need to practice dry two or three times. You must also understand that muscle memory requires 2,000-3,000 repetitions to help master a simple skill. So, at night, on your own, you must practice with a timer to ensure you are making the time standards. Occasionally, you should use video camera and record your sessions to ensure that you are not practicing or ingraining any bad habits. This is a constant cycle. Dry practice is the key. There were many times in my career in Special Operations that while in threat areas, we did not have the luxury to practice and live fire our weapons. Instead, we practiced 15-20 minutes a day against a safe wall with an empty weapon, reaffirming all the motor skills required to accomplish the act.

### Team

The team needs to implement the same protocols as the individual but at the team level. The team leader should ensure that all members are familiar with the team battle drills and that they are ingrained. Begin with a class on the drill, move to an area where you can dry practice. Once you have the concept down, move to simunitions or paintball and live role players. Then take the drill to live fire. The same training problems apply in a combat environment and that involves the time and area to practice. Team leaders can have their teams do "dry practice" by walking through buildings or garages on a reduced scale in their down time.

### Organizational

As suggested before, organization leaders should constantly work at perfecting their leadership and decision making process. They should observe and become involved in the lower level training to ensure they are aware of what their soldiers are doing and what tactics they are using. Further, they should seek to understand what actions and decisions they make to help the teams accomplish their mission. Also, they must fully appreciate the team's capabilities and limits. Finally, they should understand that it makes more sense and is more efficient to let the team complete the mission rather than to micro-manage. Only when a team leader demonstrates their incompetence, should an organizational leader step in and take control.

## SOME THOUGHTS

Boyd felt "orient" was the most important phase of his cycle. It is important to have a tactic ready, which is "oriented" to the particular situation you are in. But, I feel if you fail to see or are hesitant to decide on a course of action, you can encounter problems. While continuing to perfect the "act" phase, you must not neglect the other equally important phases of observe, orient and decide, which will cut your time navigating through the loop. Acting is important, but as much time can be cut from each of the other phases as the "Act" phase. Equally important is the ability to rapidly "see" the enemy in the observe phase and to have aggressive tactics or techniques ready in the orient phase. Finally, the decision making phase should be efficient to ensure that the act can be carried out swiftly and decisively. I prefer to cut time in all phases of the loop while training as an individual or as a group.

## KEY POINTS

- UNDERSTAND BOYD'S LOOP AND WHERE YOU CAN CUT TIME IN AN EFFORT TO MAKE YOU MORE EFFICIENT.
- UNDERSTAND YOU MUST SEE BEFORE YOU CAN SHOOT.

CHAPTER TWO

# COMBAT MINDSET

*"Take it like you own it and leave it like you sold it."*

(From a former Special Ops Sergeant Major)

- Combat Mindset Defined
- The Problems With Human Nature
- Developing A Single Combat Mindset
- Aggressiveness Is The Key
- Tactical Confidence
- Individual Mental Programing
- Team Leader Mental Programming
- Tactical Commander Mental Programming
- End Goal

## NIGHT ACTION

I watched a couple of rangers move from the Command Post (CP) to the corner of RPG alley with what appeared to be an M60 machine gun. They were only there for a few minutes when a gunman fired a rocket-propelled grenade (RPG) that impacted the corner they were using for cover. The impact of the round and subsequent explosion knocked them on their ass. A few folks from the CP came out and drug the men back in the CP. I called into the Assault Commander and told him to get the gun ships in and work the alley over. He reported to me that the Command and Control (C & C) bird was not sure where everybody was and

21

that they would not give us fire support. I was fucking pissed. I told him that there were not any friendlies up that alley. I lost my composure for a moment and switched the frequency on my radio from the working net to the command net that the C & C bird was monitoring. I called my commander in the air and told him "you get those goddamn gun ships in here right now." I relayed that I just watched two rangers get peeled off a wall and that there were not any good guys up that alley," meaning that there were not any friendly forces in that direction and to start trusting our calls for fire. After that, I switched my radio directly to the gun bird pilots and requested fire missions. They were more than happy to deliver some steel on target. Actually, they had already taken the initiative and performed some gun runs without the C & C birds approval, keeping many of the bad guys off of us. These pilots set the standard time and time again, proving that they had the highest courage, initiative, discrimination , culminating in an incredible warrior ethic. The gun bird pilots requested we mark our position and we did. Shortly all the positions were marked. Anything outside our markings were fair game for their mini-guns and rockets. They continued to tune up anyone intent on causing us problems.

Things were starting to slow down as the sun started to set. We got quiet and started using the shadows of our new home. You could hear the pilots servicing some large groups of militia who were assembling and trying to move on us. The bad guys were bringing their forces from all over the city to rendezvous points, issuing battle plans and then moving toward our positions. The pilots were engaging groups of 40-50 people at a time, clearing the street with their mini-guns, which reminded me of a chainsaw biting into wood.

Soon, the smaller enemy began to probe us using three to six person elements. I was scanning the intersection 25 meters to my left and then back to the corner of the alley about 25 meters to my right front. It was quiet, too quiet. Suddenly I heard loud jabbering and saw three individuals appear out of the alley to my right. They were dressed in dark pants and light colored shirts. I asked Tony if there were any Rangers still in that position. He said "no." I raised my car-15 from its low ready position and swept my safety to full auto. I placed my tritium front sight post on the middle thug and knew that I would sweep from center man to right and then back across the cluster. I figured Jake would take the lead guy. I braced the heavy car-15/shotgun combo against the door frame for added support. I waited a few more seconds for Jake to take the lead. Jake was 20 yards across the street in the CP, ten yards from the alley corner. Jake was on them and illuminated the first bad guy with his white light. The man stood there stunned for about a second or two with an AK in a low ready position. It looked like raccoons caught red handed in a garbage can. Jake began to service him with a few rounds of 5.56 green tip. I cut loose into the center man full auto and swept to the third and then back to the first, firing a total of about 15 rounds. Out of my peripheral view, I could see the rounds sparking off the alley wall 20 feet behind them in a tight pattern. The weight of the weapon and the supported position helped manage the recoil and keep my group tight. The next day showed a group slightly larger that a basketball in the wall behind where they had been standing.

The gunman furthest to the right in the group, went down hard and fast, while to my amazement, the first and second man moved around him and began dragging him back up the alley from where they came. The boys across the street said they did not make it far up the alley. They later reported that they could hear moaning up the alley, probably where the trio collapsed and died from loss of blood.

Tony, my Assistant Team Leader said calmly, "we should probably spread out." I said, "that's probably a good idea"...... We had taken two to three rooms of what might be considered a small house or apartment. Tony took Kim and moved through a barred window that Scott had torn out. They linked up with a fragmented group of Rangers and a couple of our guys to include a Special Operations medic. This window separated the house we were in and the next house, which connected to the alley and overlooked a crashed Black Hawk helicopter. As a buddy team, they each took a window with different fields of fire, but could see each other in the same room. One controlled the street to the North and the alley where the bird lay, and the other controlled the alley to the West where we had taken so much fire earlier.

Across the street, the CP had gotten quiet. We had several leaders there, four as a matter of fact. The assault commander and another leader of the same rank, plus two senior non-commissioned officers and an assault team were present in the courtyard and house. The second officer was along on the hit for a bit of on the job training, while the two senior non-commissioned officers ran platoon-sized elements. From my perspective, they were all relying on the one assault commander to absorb all the incoming information, process it and then make all the tactical decisions. I think these "leaders" were in a bit of shock at how quickly and violently the battle had escalated. Probably 80-90 percent of the information was going from them to the C & C bird and not to us on the ground.

At the team leader level, we were trying to tie in the now four positions of our perimeter with interlocking fire. I was on the internal channel talking with the other teams, trying to establish fields of fire and trying to ensure that we had all the approaches covered. It is tough to do at night, talking about intersections and terrain features, hoping that you and your counterpart, were looking at it the same area. We established a protocol of sorts. When we were about to shoot at incoming enemy, time permitting, you would radio and alert the force. You gave a direction, description and distance and then you would engage your threats. You would then give a brief call when you finished shooting to let everyone know what the outcome was. Sometimes the bad guys came in too quick and you just had to shoot first and then do your call. The first method helped ease your nerves, because you knew in your mind what was coming. The second method caused you to tense up until you received the status report. You did not know if the team or position might be overrun and that you might have to turn your attention elsewhere. Also, by being alerted, you could tuck back in and not be exposed to friendly or enemy fire or "bleed over" fire from the exchange.

During this and other actions, our internal radios enabled us to effectively communicate and keep the force informed. The one technical problem we faced was that of battery life. As most law enforcement personnel are aware, communications is one of the biggest weaknesses in the system. Ours were no different. Our batteries were a rechargeable type that did not last long when transmitting. For years we had asked for a disposable lithium type battery that you could carry in an emergency and talk on for days, when things got tough. Hopefully our troops have them now, but they still may be facing the same problems. To ensure constant radio communications, one person on the buddy team would turn their radio off and receive the information verbally from his partner to save battery life. After a few hours, they would switch radios and the other man would turn his on. This went on all night.

Everyone was on edge and my biggest fear was that of being overrun. I went through a mental checklist of my equipment, my "layered offense" as I termed it and how I was going to do business if the bad guys came at us in mass. I checked all my rifle magazines and ensured that I could easily get to them should we get hit with a wave of enemy bodies. I thought about stacking them on the window ledge next to the door, but that would limit my mobility. I would be stuck there in that position, good or bad. I chose to keep them on my body. I checked my shotgun rounds and still had the 30 or so I had brought in with me. Should my rifle fail or I run out of ammo, I would go to my shotgun and #4 buck. Should I need to transition from my shotgun, I would go to my pistol. I had one mag in the gun and two on my belt. My final check was my last frag and my knife. I had one large fragmentation grenade left. I would save my frag for a large group of fighters or to clean some hard cases from out around a corner. My knife was for if it got up close and personal. Before I got to that point, I would prefer to pick-up an enemy AK assault rifle, as it always had a soft spot in my heart for the reliability and knock down power of its cartridge.

As the night wore on, Tony and Kim started to get some trigger time. They would engage the bad guys here and there, allowing them to come down a wall to an undefendable position and then open up with a 40mm grenade to the front and 5.56 on both sides with great results. At one point, I was scanning the intersection to my left, one that was supposedly covered by a sister team, when this bad guy comes walking down the center of the street. I was trying to put my light cover back on my rifle gun light when I had a white light accidental discharge (AD). Simply put, I screwed up and my white light flashed the ground. Instead of going straight, this recon scout made the last bad decision in his life and turned toward us and started walking down the center of our street. He was doing a recon, trying to pinpoint our positions so he could later bring back his friends with RPG's to try and root us out. I pulled my pistol out and started tracking him, putting my tritium sights center mass of his right side. He was a big guy, over 6 foot and stocky. Looking at the background of my target, I would be shooting almost directly into the CP and my muzzle flash would be exposed to three different directions. So, I got on my radio and called Jake and told him to take the guy out when he leaves the perimeter. Jake had a great position at his gate that concealed their positions from all angles but one. Jake acknowledged and let him walk about 15 feet and fired one round that struck him in the lower left of his back and exited the right front side, the bullet "poofing" out of his shirt as it exited his body. The guy spun around and looked at Jake for a second at which time Jake serviced him with 2-3 more rounds in the chest, dropping him in his tracks. This bad guy dropped in the wrong spot and later became a "speed bump" for some of our recovery and convoy vehicles.

Immediately a voice came over the radio, one of the senior NCO's in the CP saying, "I don't think he had a gun." I thought to myself, what a dumb "mother-fucker." He still has not switched over to combat. Just then, as I was scanning back to my left, another guy was walking down the center of the street where the first one had come from. I raised my rifle and was tracking him with my front sight and I had a good squeeze going on my trigger, when bam, the guy dropped. A sister team leader who I thought had that area covered, had just opened a window and saw this guy in the middle of the street, probably 20 feet away. He tagged him with several rounds and immediately got on the radio saying, "you gotta tell me when these guys are coming in." I laughed and told him that I thought he had that area covered. It was covered and

I did not take it for granted that he had it. Things tend to look different in the day than at night. Lesson learned.

An hour or so later, the two deceased recon scouts' friends decided to come pay us a visit. The light from the moon was so bright, it produced night shadows. These were cast from buildings, trees, etc. I was watching the intersection to the left again, even though it was "again" covered and caught sight of a Somali gunman on a knee, poking his AK around the corner. He fired one shot down the wall toward the area of the CP. I told the guys in the CP to tuck in and hold tight. The ground going to the CP was sloping down and the round went way above their heads. This guy was reconning by fire. This is an old military technique where you shoot and then see who shoots back.

We all held our fire and he got a little braver. He crawled on his hands and knees halfway down the wall with his AK tucked under his arm, moving like a jungle cat, slow and precise. He used the shadows as he moved and I viewed his movement as a work of art. He moved up to a point about 20 feet from the CP, looked hard for a moment, turned around and went back to the corner from which he came. I told Scott to get ready, we were going to get some business. We took up a high/low position when all of a sudden the corner where the bad guy was exploded in gunfire, one sided of course.

It seems the other team spotted him and it turned out to be five more of his friends getting ready to move on the CP. Our sister team worked them over good, putting rounds into all of them. Again, they managed to drag their dead and wounded back up the street. Once first light came, there were no bodies to be seen.

## AFTER ACTION COMMENTS

### Sustain:

- Continue to require individual initiative at the team member and team leader level. Ensure that they are "thinkers that are shooters and shooters that are thinkers.
- Ensure the communication process continues at the individual and team level.

- Know when to change from a surgical mindset to a combat mindset. Discuss this before you go into harm's way. Otherwise, as a leader let them know when to shoot by setting the example.

### Improve

- Don't layer fire support. The soldiers on the ground know who is shooting at them and from where. Generally fire support gets screwed up when you get a third and fourth party involved.
- Senior leadership needs to get proactive, check the perimeter and support the teams in the fight. Again, lead by example.

## COMBAT MINDSET DEFINED

"An aggressive combat mindset is possessed by people who can screen out distractions while under great stress, focus on the mission and willing to go into harm's way; against great odds if necessary." Hemingway might have described it as "grace under pressure." Simply put, we must be able to maintain our focus and composure and not allow fear or stress to cause us to make stupid or sloppy mistakes. Combat Mindset sets the stage for all components of this book. Without it, you will be unable to employ positive and decisive leadership in critical situations.

The problems that affect combat mindset lies with human nature. When the sound of shots ring out, the average person will stop and cringe, physically if not mentally. As soon as their mind registers what the shots actually are, i.e., gunfire, their mind will kick in the flight or fight self-preservation response. For the average human, the urge is to flee. Special Operations soldiers, to include law enforcement tactical personnel, must act contrary to human nature and must control their fear and channelize it into "controlled aggression" and move around and sometimes into the fire. This even applies to the average police patrolman on the street responding to the report of an "active shooter" call, where a gunman is wading into innocent people, shooting them like sheep. Military, law enforcement tactical personnel and patrol officers need to be mentally, physically and tactically ready to wade into a fight, bypassing injured and dying innocent people to quickly and efficiently neutralize a threat so more innocent people will not die.

Developing "Controlled Aggression" is a key factor in combat mindset. That is, channelizing their fear, anger and anxiety into a focused mental package. Channelizing and controlling this energy is routinely what military individuals term as "high speed." They use it to describe the caliber, efficiency or speed a soldier or team operates. High speed in my dictionary is the ability to apply the basics on demand the first time in a high stress situation. Some people falsely think it counts after a dozen rehearsals. The real people who wear the "high speed" badge can execute a live fire explosive breach cold hit on a target with an unknown floor plan and not kill or injure themselves or any innocents.

More times than I wish to count, I have witnesses individuals with "uncontrolled aggression," screw up missions, tactical problems and routine combat actions. Instead of donning their equipment for the right reasons, with the understanding that it takes thousands of hours to attain a basic skill level, some special operations soldiers wear the gear for the CDI (chicks dig it) factor and forget that the reality is that it is hard work. Success will require countless rehearsals and constant maintenance training to hone your individual and collective skills. Some individuals tend to rely on their physical prowess to solve tactical problems, leaving their brain somewhere far behind. Combat is a thinking man's game and you need to rely on skill versus luck to ensure your survival. No matter what you problem is, you have to first get your mind right to ensure your survival. If you find luck, embrace it, but don't rely on it.

## THE PROBLEMS OF HUMAN NATURE

The mindset I choose to use, served me well. Through the years I was able to watch fellow soldiers and law enforcement individuals and see what worked and did not work. I grew up in an era of Vietnam veterans who recently separated from service and entered the law enforcement arena. They were a great crew, confident, professional, no nonsense guys who did not take crap from the low life's or dirtballs of the community.

The other side of this coin is the shit talkers I have run into during my life. I have come to the conclusion that braggers and loud mouths are the first to crumble in a high stress situation. I venture to say that their outward projection is a smoke screen for a lack of confidence. I will not generally lump them into the "coward" category, but they are close. I have seen too many shit-talking leaders crumble when the first bullet snaps by their head. Their balls shrink from their self-perceived bowling ball size, to that of BB's. I equate loud talk as foreshadowing of failure. This is my mathematical view of boasting.

Loud talk = failure = impotence/cowardice

As for ego's, leave your ego behind in your wall locker or better yet, permanently deflate it. Learn to focus on the task at hand and solve one problem at a time. Should you make a mistake, admit it and concentrate on how to fix it. All an over inflated ego will do is to confirm you are an asshole and make you look like a pussy when you crumble under the stress of combat. Few will have sympathy for you and hopefully you will not get too many men killed because you are too ignorant to listen, take suggestions or fix your mistakes. Don't talk about doing something, do it. It is the only way to make believers of non-believers. An old martial arts instructor said, "Believe half of what you see and none of what you hear." There is much truth in this. Unfortunately, I have run into to too many individuals in life who talk a good game, but cannot perform to their level of boasting.

As a final point in this section I would like to tie in a final point General Patton mentioned in his book, "War as I Knew It."

> "If we take the generally accepted definition of bravery as a quality which knows not fear, I have never seen a brave man. All men are frightened. The more intelligent they are, the more they are frightened. The courageous man is the man who forces himself, in spite of his fear, to carry on. Discipline, pride, self-respect, self-confidence, and the love of glory are attributes which will make a man courageous even when he is afraid."

The point I would like to make is that the more one develops their mind and situational awareness, the more control they will need in combat to sort out all the information being processed. Call this courage or call it a "combat focus," it is something you will need to help you process the combat information that your senses absorb. My idea of a combat focus is two fold, consisting of a soft and a hard focus. Our soft-focus is a relaxed vision that I routinely operate in and consists of looking at the big picture, a landscape so to speak. The hard or detailed focus is where you pick out a point on that landscape, such a bush or rock to focus your attention and "see" a particular point. Combat and Close Quarter Battle (CQB) requires the ability to change from soft to hard focus and back again almost instantly. In combat, you are continually scanning the environment or field of view for threats. When traveling down a street under fire, you're looking for the obvious, people with guns, muzzle flashes, etc. As you scan for the obvious, you start looking hard at places that can conceal a shooter, dark windows, doorways and roof lines. You are continually going back and forth through this visual process. You might see a flash from a window, zoom in on it for a second, put a few rounds on it and then pull back to a soft focus of the entire terrain again. You might go back to the window again, just to ensure the threat does not reappear.

Lets add something more to this picture. When moving and shooting, bullets are also coming your way. Some bullets might be going high and you just hear the report of the weapon, others rounds may go by your head and snap or crack as they go by. Others still may spark or poof the ground around your feet. This is where Patton's comments hit home for me. I know that as I became more situationally aware, my mind attempted to absorb and process all this information. The key is to sort out what is critical information and what is not. I found the "air balls,' were nothing to get excited about. Yes, someone is shooting your way, this does happen in combat. More likely they are either a bad shot or just slinging lead. You need to go into combat expecting people to shoot at you and not be naïve to this danger.

The rounds that should be getting you excited are the ones that are cracking by your head or sparking the ground next to your feet. These should be sending a signal to your brain saying that someone is zeroed in on you and doing their best to try and kill you. Your options are simple, seek a better route to get to your destination or get some cover. Sending enough lead your way, the bad guy will eventually hit you if you continue your same approach. Even if they only hit you with one out of ten rounds, it still will hurt.

# DEVELOP YOUR COMBAT MINDSET

I know I am being redundant, but I will hammer this point again. You must firmly believe in what you are doing and why you are doing it. It can be for your country, the organization, your team or your buddy next to you. It can be that inner drive that says don't quit and do your best. Whatever, motivates you, you need to harness it and keep it strong in its place. Reflect on it as needed to keep your energies channelized for the time that will come for you to earn your keep. The stronger your belief the stronger your mindset.

This resolve or strength will also help ensure your survival. With it, you will train harder and push farther than someone who does not have it. Use this strength to develop your own personal beast and then keep it in its place. Some folks may look at me funny when I use this analogy, but it is simple. When you are confronted with a desperate and possibly lethal situation, your physiological and mental system kicks in. Breathing, heart rate, adrenaline, all come into play. Your fight or flight response also factors into the equation. The key is not to figure the best way to run away, but to figure out the most efficient and violent way to remedy the problem at hand. Learning to channelize the energy into positive action and thought is the real key.

Develop your personal "Beast," for these times. Everyone has that switch they can throw that will take them to another level or fighting plane. Go to a place where you can become emotionless and totally focused. You must have the ability to be situationally aware so you can wade efficiently into multiple threats and be successful. Still keep the emotion harnessed for that little "umph" you may need should the situation become desperate. I was able to develop this at a young age and then harness it for future use. You can use it while doing live fire CQB, ramping yourself to a mental level where you are conscious of everything going on around you, explosive charges going off, shooting, shotgun breaching, flash bangs, assaulters screaming and putting people down in the next room. You can learn to focus through this and do your job and turn it on when you need to. Your job may be as simple as clearing a single empty room or as complex as dealing with a room containing multiple friendly innocents, who at the same time are running, bleeding and screaming. You must maintain your focus and composure while swiftly and efficiently putting surgical rounds into the right target.

One mindset that I kept firmly implanted was that of the "Layered Offense." Everyone and their brother want to talk about being defensive. Generally, defense does not win personal or collective battles. In my mind, I always wanted to stay focused and in the fight. I used the knife on my belt as a useful cutting tool, but it served a dual purpose. I would mentally program it as part of my layered offense. I had my rifle to employ as my primary weapon. If it malfunctioned or I was out of ammo, I would go to my pistol. Once my pistol was out of action, I would try and then pick up an enemy weapon to use. If none were close, I would then go to my knife. The knife I carried was virtually indestructible and it was kept sharp. The only part of it that could fail was the person wielding it-me. I knew deep down that I had to maintain my belief, my skills and my physical condition to survive. This kept it simple and in perspective for me. Fortunately, no one has ever made it past my rifle in combat, but should I have needed to, there would be no hesitation in transitioning to my next weapon system. This mindset could be termed a "weapon loop," where I always knew where to go and find my next lethal system to employ. Keeping it simple, kept me fluid and efficient.

Once I developed this layered offensive mindset, I had to weigh being fast and sloppy or methodical and precise in my tactical ways. I chose the later, erring on the side of being methodical and precise versus fast and sloppy. Instructors I had in the past, always reminded us that, "Smooth is Fast". We were continually pushed to be precise and in control.

Furthermore, I developed one mindset for all tactical situations. Special operations and law enforcement tactical teams usually have four or five standard high-risk missions they are tasked to perform. In the law enforcement arena, they are, hostage rescue, high-risk warrant, search warrant and barricaded persons. What is the constant for each mission? They are dangerous and you can get shot at while doing them. I recommend that you develop a simple and aggressive mindset that will work for each mission. I developed my personal combat mindset to help me deliver efficient lethal force on demand. I went into every mission with the belief that someone was going to shoot at me and I expected it. Failure to do this will leave you in a mentally unprepared condition to deal with the violence of action that someone might bring upon you. You will also be too late to ratchet up your aggressiveness once the bullet started flying.

"I am going to fucking destroy you," is the thought I firmly and quietly placed into my mind along with a game face of focused determination when I was preparing for a combat mission or doing rehearsals with role players. I treated both rehearsals and combat the same for simplicity's sake. As for role players, they come in two types, professional and standard. The professional role players are the ones that have been role players before and like to try to get the drop on an assaulter or good guy. Some will push you and try and control a situation during an assault, creating additional chaos for you to deal with. This can be as simple as acting out a script of a panicking passenger or a smart ass that wants to verbally challenge you during the scenario. It is important to gain physical, emotional and mental control of the situation as rapidly as possible. Once you get security and neutralize any obvious threats, you need to immediately deal with these kinds of people. Failure to do this will make your job much more difficult. If you "educate or tune-up" the problem child as rapidly as possible, especially in front of their peers, you will make believers of non-believers. I remember one time where a role player was screaming uncontrollably and rushing around, causing a disturbance. Four operators did not want to touch her because she was a female. She had them on the run. She was starting to take control of the scenario and other role players were looking to see what they could get away with. I have seen this apprehension before in the ranks of the military because the environment they are raised in, lacks females and our society has brought us up never to strike women. At the time of this scenario, there were 20 plus hostages watching to see what was going to happen. I lost my sense of humor for a moment and grabbed the person by the back of the head and the throat and while temporarily denying her oxygen, whispered into her ear "if you fuck-up my assault, I am going to break your back right fucking now." "I asked her if she understood and she nodded slightly with her head and eyes. I then dumped her in a seat on her head and asked the other 20 individuals if they had any issues they would like to discuss. It was uneventful after that. I am not proud that I had to tune-up a female, but it was my job as I saw it and I learned to treat everyone the same, as they can all kill you equally dead. Finally, rest assured that all males present were confident that we would be equally as decisive should they wish to start trouble.

## AGGRESSIVENESS IS THE KEY

I usually begin my combat mindset module with a talk about aggressiveness. This is the key to success.

Your mindset and attitude <u>should not</u> be:

- Passive
- Reactive
- Nor neutral, but rather proactive and aggressive. ACT vs. REACT.

I preach in my classes that there exists a pool of aggressiveness in any combat situation. Either you will take it and use it, or your opponent will. The choice is yours. Chaos exists on the battlefield and has more effect on the mind and perception than on reality. Chaos can be used to describe the combined sensory overload that affects you during raids or combat operations. Our job is to bring order to chaos. Sometimes we need to bring our own brand of chaos to help establish order. Imagine if you will, an environment with brilliant flashes and the concussion of explosions going off near you, people shooting, doors being shotgun breached, distraction devices flashing and booming. This is chaos, induced chaos. This chaos helps you to do your job safely and efficiently. You must learn to understand it, be aware of it and let it pass by your senses. You use it to control everyone on your target. Once you gain control, you can ease back as your target audience dictates. In a Hostage Rescue scenario, everyone should be physically, emotionally and mentally dominated from the instant they lay eyes on the team. I want them scared to death upon our entry with individuals curled into a fetal position. This quickly sorts out who is serious and who is not. Fetal positions are a good indicator of compliant hostages. I joke in class that they can always get therapy later, but they are alive to get the therapy.

Most of the time the chaos you bring in will take the fight out of the most hardened opponent. I remember other men recounting instances where all the bad guys on the target were proned out after the first explosion went off. They did not want to play against guys who were serious about doing business. I also remember a raid where the father had his family lined up in front of the breach point in a line and held their infant out as a shield in front of them. This happened not once, but twice during one operation. These guys were supposed to be high-ranking officers in their militia. In effect, they were low life cowards. American's wonder what separates us from other countries, races and ethnic groups. It's is how we cherish and protect our children. The thought process in other countries is that life is cheap and they can make more kids. These infants and children are those who are sacrificed first when times get tough.

Occasionally, you will assault into a hard target where everyone will not surrender and throw their hands up. For this, I always believed in developing and going in with one mindset, the mindset that it is going to be a hard fight. I always prepare mentally for that one guy that is going to fight back and try and fight through you, the guy that you are going to have to shoot to pieces in order to stop. It has happened before and it will happen again in the future. Law enforcement officers occasionally run into an individual with a fixed combat mindset and they literally have to shoot these folks apart to get them to stop their aggressive actions.

## TACTICAL CONFIDENCE

By developing simple and effective drills that will apply to a majority of your missions, you will develop a confidence that is instilled in the lowest team member to the team leader. Why is it important? Simple, if your men do not believe in the tactics they are going to employ, they will generally fall apart once the shooting starts. Also, if your tactics are based on the "best case" scenario, versus worse case scenario, your men will have too much to deal with mentally once things start going wrong.

All of us have the talent, expertise, experience and resources to develop simple and effective "battle plans" that will work on all missions. For example, moving from a drop off point from a van or moving to a target on foot is basically the same wherever you go. If someone is going to shoot at you, your tactics should address this and it should work for all missions. Simply put, getting shot at is getting shot at. It is the same whether you are on a hostage rescue mission, a high-risk warrant, search warrant or barricaded person type mission. For all these missions, I teach a simple drill called a "Tactical Flare," where the men move into positions that spread them out, away from the gun fire, allowing them to all shoot safely and bring all their firepower to bear on the threat. Generally, I see movement formations to the initial breach point of a target consisting of a line of ducks where only the first man can safely shoot. Should they encounter a suspect or take fire, the team is relying on the lead officer to solve the problem. This is in effect a one on one gunfight. For starters, I put a minimum of two men up front with two guns and two sets of eyes for a faster response time. Once verbal or non-verbal communication (shooting) is initiated by the point personnel, the remainder of the team deploys into offensive firing positions.

This does several things. First, it encourages men to respond aggressively forward and to not react or to maintain a neutral "wait and see" posture. Next, it gets the team spread out and out of the bad guy's cone of fire. Further, it mentally overwhelms the threat because now he is not facing one lone officer, he has multiple aggressive movers to contend with as well as several weapons pointed at him. You create a "reactionary gap" in the subjects mind and then you exploit it. There is nothing like good old fashioned aggressive action. Using this technique, the officers will have a better visual angle and should the officers decide to shoot, they can all do so safely. I learned long ago, that more guns will make the bad person go away faster, either mentally or physically.

Let's throw in a variable into the above situation, that being an officer down scenario. If an officer gets shot during the drill, what changes? Nothing. The team will neutralize the threat and then recover the officer once it is safe to do so. I see too many times where officers try and strong point the downed officer. By doing this, they become a bullet magnet and all the bad guy has to do is to shoot into a "clump" of officers. By retreating, they will also have to deal with the threat again. I hate paying for the same ground twice. In my view it is safer and more efficient to solve the problem the first time and recover the officer once you own the turf.

By fighting through the problem, we have one drill that will work on all missions. It is simple, safe, easy to learn and does not change from hit to hit. The key point is who we should be designing this drill for. Should it be the 12 year Special Ops or Swat veteran or the new member of the team? It should be the newest and weakest link on the team. Keep it simple. We now have a drill for exterior movement with few variables. Once practiced and mastered, we need to now focus on developing a simple drill for your breach point, hallways, rooms, etc. By keeping it simple and easy to remember, it will transition to other tactical situations with ease.

Developing scenario based drills will also help combat the fear of the unknown. Fear of the unknown is one of the biggest problems encountered when training new team members. Their mind is racing with all the possible scenarios that they can run into. It is controlled by training on realistic worse case scenario contingencies and having a plan to deal with them. First, expect to be shot at and have the confidence that your basic battle drills will adequately handle the threats. Next, make fear of the unknown a non-issue by knowing what you're going to do in a positive, aggressive manner. This is termed anticipation mindset. For example, once officers practice the flare, I run five or six different basic worse case scenarios with role players and see if the drill will effectively manage them. I video each drill and review it in a classroom environment. We then practice our problem areas again and smooth out our actions.

I learned long ago when I was deployed overseas, that many times we are going to come across people with guns. We can't shoot them all, but we can figure out the ones that plan on using them against us. These are the real threats we need to be concerned with and have a plan for dealing with those individuals. I know that action is faster than reaction, so start by developing a "tactical package" that will give your team a tactical confidence and edge in how they perform a mission and deal with these individuals, both mentally and physically.

# INDIVIDUAL MENTAL PROGRAMMING-
# DEVELOP A "FIGHT THROUGH MENTALITY"

Coupled with the points brought up earlier in this chapter, are a few more points that need to be added to your survival toolbox. First, believe in the cause, yourself and your team. Probably one of the greatest fears is that of letting down your buddy or your team in combat. A proper mission focus along with having the proper tactical confidence in your battle drills will help eliminate this fear. If your tactics are sound and you believe that they will keep you relatively safe while delivering devastating fire to your opponent, you will have less fear and apprehension when going into harm's way.

Next, there is no problem with being scared. It is natural. How can you channelize that fear? Easy. Look at the technical aspects of the battle and do the math. For example, lets look at getting shot. If you have done any amount of range fire, you know how hard it is to hit a stationary target, let alone a moving target. You must first ensure your rifle is zeroed and practice. The same rule applies to the bad guys and they generally don't have the training and marksmanship abilities you do. Next, if you use cover, it makes the bad guy work hard at getting an accurate shot at you. So, use cover and decrease your chances of being hit.

Most importantly, develop a "fight through" mentality. Do not dwell on dying. Focus on your training and what you are going to do to ensure your survival. So you get hit. Big deal. Look at the statistics of those dying from gunshot wounds. They are not that impressive. Generally, you can reach some type of definitive care in a few minutes or it can reach you. Before you reach this care, who is best person to start treatment on you? You are. Start by getting your mind right and being pissed off that some low life turd shot you and focus your mind toward survival. Do this by ensuring the bad guy is dead and then start your self-aid. As a realist, I carry medical scissors and several bandages readily accessible on my belt. I know by experience that I can get shot by the enemy or by friendly personnel. Should this happen, I will do my best to fight through, neutralize the threat and let my buddy know that I am hit. I am then going to cut my own clothing, expose the wound and come to grips with my own injury. I will pack it or tie it off with a tourniquet if time permits so as not to take team members away from the team and their ultimate goal of securing the target. I know they will come back for me once the area is secure. The more that I can do to treat myself, the less they have to do for me. Implementing this thought process will start kicking your survival mindset into high gear.

You can always take the other approach and roll your eyes back in you head and go towards the light. I prefer not to take this approach. You might make it sooner than you expect. When training with simunitions or paintball and you get hit, fight through. Why? We have trained our soldiers for years to fall down, quit, give up once they are hit during training scenarios. This is self-destructive and will cause you problems in combat. You're actually training soldiers to give up at the slightest pain or discomfort. I have witnessed soldiers with minor wounds mentally shut down in combat because they have trained that way during years of battle drills and rehearsals. For medical training, you can induce casualties, but do it by telling a soldier ahead of time that he is part of a medical scenario. Never allow a soldier or law enforcement officer to quit on their own. This will start a bad habit that may cultivate hesitation or result in a soldier or officer giving up in the heat of battle where they generally could have survived. **Finally, if you think you're going to die, get pissed and plan on taking some of the bad guys with you. Do your best to ensure this happens.**

## TEAM LEADER MENTAL PROGRAMMING

The Team Leader should strive to cultivate and demonstrate the same mental attitude as the individual and project this to the team. Your job as a team leader is to "live the example" for all to see and aspire to be. We are not talking about perfection, but darn close. The individuals you are going to lead into harm's way need to have the confidence and belief that your priorities are right. That priority is to fight smart and hard and bring all team members back at all costs. The team should know this and it should be talked out prior to going into harm's way.

The team leader is the first line of fighting leadership. If he has a target of opportunity, he engages it in a rapid and efficient manner as would any member of the team. This may not sound like much, but it can make a world of difference in combat. If your team has not been bloodied together, or been bloodied at all, they may be hesitant to shoot when the time comes due to complicated rules of engagement (ROE). You being a new leader could cause this hesitation among a team. A single act of you aggressively engaging threat targets will pass as a wave of silent condonement to your team that you mean business and that it is time for them to get some trigger time. If I was a new team member and saw my team leader engaging targets, I would feel a slight bit of guilt that I was not doing my job. When you see the boss shooting, you know things are serious and you should be getting after it.

S.L.A. Marshall wrote about this type of action in his book, "Men Against Fire." It is an incredible piece of work. One incident rang true when Marshall described a leader that would come along and yell at his men to shoot and then leave. Once this leader left, the men would stop shooting. He described another leader that would come into position next to his men and start shooting at enemy targets and talk to the guys. The men would start engaging targets and once the leader left, they would continue to engage the enemy. I can attribute this action to two reasons. First, if my boss is firing, it must be serious and I better do my part. The other reason might deal with today's civilianized combatants and the right or wrong thoughts of engaging people in civilian clothes. Again, if the boss is doing it, they must be bad guys.

On the other side of the coin, each Special Ops type person is required to be a shooter and a thinker. I can remember not shooting more times in combat or high risk confrontations because it was not the right thing to do at the time. We were raised to be surgical and actually avoided more fights than we got into, because it was the smart thing to do. I remember one incident when our vehicles were surrounded in a foreign country by 15-20 pissed off government troops, some with fingers on the triggers and the safety off, muzzles stuck in the windows of our vehicles. It was not in our best interest to escalate, so we remained calm during the encounter and allowed the situation to de-escalate. Had one of the government troops had an accidental discharge because of their poor weapon handling, it would have been a different story. We would probably have won the fight, but we would have had casualties because of the close distance and amount of guns involved. This is where you have to leave your ego and pride in the rear. They may be booger-eaters, but they are booger eaters with lots of guns.

Where the combat mindset issue may come into question is where a seasoned team inherits an unproven team leader. All the team leader can do is live the example and set the standard in all training and combat. You should do this as the opportunity presents itself and you will develop the respect you need to effectively lead your element. You need to earn the team's respect every day and continue to pay your dues. The team, if mature and professional, should not hold that you were in the wrong place at the wrong time and did not see any action in the past. Generally, the team will watch you and see your decision making process and if they determine that you cannot make a hard decision in peacetime or in training under no stress, they will conclude that you are spineless and will crumble in combat or a high stress situation. They are probably right.

## TACTICAL COMMANDER MENTAL PROGRAMMING

The mindset or attitude of the Tactical Commander should generally stay the same as the individual and the team leader. Hopefully they have the same aggressiveness as the lower leaders, but things have a tendency of changing. Routinely Special Ops leaders at this level, the troop level, are only given a short time to work with and interact with the soldiers. Generally two years and they are off to another assignment, usually administrative and as far away from the shooters as possible. Two years is generally enough time to learn the missions and SOP's to become an effective and integrated part of the machine.

Much of the problem with commander's combat mindset mental programming is that they are rarely faced with the immediate threats and violence of action that the troops face on a daily basis. Generally, the troops come in first and create secure safe havens for the command to operate, a buffer zone if you will. With this buffer zone, many times a commander loses, or should I say, never develops a "violence of action" mindset necessary to be effective in the arena. They usually resort to a "Management Roll" in leadership. They are insulated from the hard decisions of combat and many times lose touch with the reality of battle.

Solving this problem is easy. Longer times spent working with the troops is the key. Ideally, a commander should be brought up from the troop level to ensure they have a proven and developed combat mindset. Too often in the Army's current leadership doctrine, leaders prove themselves once upon their graduation from their officer basic course and then many pursue a free ride in their career, never having to prove their mettle again. Soldiers and team leaders are required to prove their combat mindset on a daily basis under the scrutiny of their peers. Officers are not. And the further officers climb up the chain, the more insulated they become from the harsh realities of combat.

Effective combat leaders should require their troops to be aggressive in combat and hold them to it in training. Oversee training and hold the personnel accountable by being at the training. When you can smell the gunpowder you're getting close. Don't get in their way, but be close enough to ensure they have the right mindset and aggressiveness needed to accomplish the mission. If they don't, it is up to you to instill it in them or fire a team leader.

As with the team leader, the tactical commander should be under the scrutiny of their bosses who require a higher standard because more lives are riding on their action or inaction. This is where decision-making should become critical. If a commander cannot make a hard decision in peacetime and in training, he will not do it under the stress of combat. Although this should be addressed and remedied, it is too often overlooked. Many of our high-ranking leaders seek out and promote those who do not rock the boat or make waves. As discussed at the team leader level, troops should ask the command level leader how far they are going to go to bring them back. In simple terms, "how many people are you going to kill, to get us home?" If the leader cannot look you in the eye on this issue and give you a firm response, beware, you're headed for trouble. These types of leaders are the ones that will crumble under the stress of combat and will try and cover all their mistakes once the battle is over.

## END GOAL

We must be able to apply the appropriate degree of force and discrimination… demonstrating a complete business like attention to detail and if necessary, we must be able to kill with ruthless efficiency.

## COMBAT MINDSET KEY POINTS

- DEVELOP ONE COMBAT MINDSET FOR ALL SITUATIONS.
- DEVELOP AND PRACTICE YOUR LAYERED OFFENSE.
- PRACTICE FIGHTING THROUGH AND NEVER GIVING UP.
- HAVE TACTICAL CONFIDENCE IN YOUR DRILLS AND TACTICS.

# CHAPTER THREE

# INDIVIDUAL LEADERSHIP

*"War is an ugly thing, but not the ugliest of things. The decayed and degraded state of moral and patriotic feeling that thinks that nothing is worth war is much worse. The person who has nothing for which he is willing to fight, nothing which is more important than his own personal safety, is a miserable creature and has no chance of being free unless made and kept so by the exertions of better men than himself."*

John Stuart Mill

- WHY LEAD?
- ATTAINING COMBAT EFFICIENCY
- PERSONAL EFFORT
- BE SIMPLE AND EFFICIENT AND COMPETE WITH YOURSELF FIRST
- GET OUT OF YOUR COMFORT ZONE AND DEVELOP MENTAL TOUGHNESS
- TRADITIONAL AND UNTRADITIONAL APPROACHES TO ATTAINING LEADERSHIP GOALS AND COMMON COUNTER PRODUCTIVE ATTITUDES
- THE JOURNEY OR DESTINATION

## MOVEMENT TO THE CRASH SITE

We were on top of the target building and AK's and RPG's were starting to fly. We had just secured the target and rounded up 22 of the bad guys and were awaiting the convoys arrival to exfil them. We got the call that a Black Hawk helicopter had been shot down and it was 300-500 meters away from our position. At the time I did not realize it, but I had watched the CSAR (Combat Search and Rescue) force fast rope on to the crash site. As they were fast roping in, an RPG hit the tail boom with a bang. I watched the bird shutter and waiver a bit while shards and strips of steel shot out the back area of the bird near the tail boom. The pilot did a heroic job of holding the bird in place while all the members of the team made it to the ground. Panicking and lifting off would mean almost certain death to those still sliding down the rope.

The assault force commander passed the word to the team leaders that we would be moving on foot. The movement order was Rangers in front, us in the middle and Rangers in the rear. The enemy volume of fire had increased and I thought to myself, "this is going to be fun," in my "dry humor" thought process. I briefed my team (myself Tony, Scott and Kim) and we stacked in the courtyard by the interior of the gate. When our lead teams flowed out of the gate, we moved, staying on the left side of the street.

Initially, most of the fire was coming from straight ahead toward us. As we approached the first intersection, you could strain your eyes and see the AK rounds sparking and skipping off the walls across the street, traveling from left to right. We would post our near side cover and wait a few seconds for a lull in the fire. Generally a soldier with an AK will have to reload after 20-30 seconds of sustained semi-automatic fire. This is the time to take back the street and get your guys across. When the lull took place, the cover man would roll out on their own or he would get tapped out. Once he started his suppressive fire, we would dash across and pick up a cover position on the other side. Generally, I would start my run not at the corner, but several feet back so when I hit the intersection, I was at a dead run while in the kill zone. I wanted to cut my exposure time and not give the bad guy the chance to get on his gun and track me. Wearing the heavy Kevlar vest and loaded with ammunition, you needed the extra few paces to hit full speed. Also, it was a bit easier on your joints and ligaments to get the mass moving. In my case, it was like getting a heavy diesel truck moving. A diesel truck may not be fast out of the gate, but they can cruise at high speeds for a long time. We leap-frogged the entire team across the kill zone. Occasionally, we would also work with another team if they needed the support.

We continued to take fire from the front, rounds popping and cracking as they passed far and near. A few steps ahead and to my left, a Ranger took a leg wound and crumpled to the ground. To my amazement, no less than four to five soldiers stopped to try and help him. I yelled at them to keep moving and to let the medics handle it. My rational is that if he got shot there, we can get shot there and it would be better to move forward and neutralize whoever did the shooting. This way we would all be safe and the casualty could be treated within relative safety.

Adding to the stress, the formation became a stop-and-go procession, reminding me of one who would play an accordion. As the fire was increasing, the lead elements were having a difficult time maintaining their momentum. Being in the middle and the back of the formation sucked, as we could not suppress to our front because of the friendlies up there. We had to move right or left and hope to avoid one of the incoming rounds that had missed everyone up front. Some of the Special Ops boys got pissed and moved to the middle of the street to lay down some fire to the front. Evidently they felt the lead folks were not putting enough rounds out.

We looked at the terrain and street we were moving on and it began to narrow. I took my team to the right side of the street and was on one knee looking over a three-foot wall at a house 15 yards away. In the driveway, laying on his stomach next to a car, was a Somali moaning and a thick blood trail flowing away from his chest. I thought about shooting him again, but I knew he was out of action and I did not want to waste my ammo. I was worried more about the house 15 yards on the other side of him, a perfect place for a shooter to come out and engage us.

Glancing to my left across the street, I thought, "I wish these dumb mother-fuckers would get moving." I watched a "little bird" swoop in extraordinarily low from right to left at about 30 feet off a roof top and throw a green smoke grenade down the street to my left, about two blocks away. I knew that the crash site was in that area. At this point the formation was a bogged down column that had lost its momentum. I shouted to someone to tell the Assault Force Commander to follow me and curtly told the team "on me," and began our movement down the left side of the intersecting street toward the site. We moved from cover to cover as best we could. Sometimes we could find a wall or outcropping to hide behind, but they were few and far between. When needed, we kicked in a door, cleared the initial rooms of the building, to create a safe haven out of the fire and to catch our breath and hastily plan our next move. We did just that about 35 meters up the left side of the street. Once the initial clear was finished, Kim told me he had been hit. I pulled my tanto style knife out of its kydex sheath and plucked the BDU jacket away from his skin and carefully sliced his uniform open in the area of his left kidney. Looking for a wound, I found it and it looked like a high-speed entrance wound that from a pencil eraser sized pieced of shrapnel. It had swelled up about the diameter of a golf ball and was sufficiently swollen and did not bleed. I told him it was not bad and he prepared for our next move. He immediately got back into the stack and got his mind on the game.

At this point, we were pushing forward into a hail of rifle, machine gun Rocket Propelled Grenade (RPG) fire. AK rounds were popping through the air similar to the sound of a dry sticks being snapped. Occasionally you would catch the dust "poof or spark" out of the corner of your eye when one impacted close to you. RPG's were coming in every 20-30 seconds and they would rock our world. You could see the orange glow of the rocket motor pushing the drifting dark mass toward you. A sharp explosion and deafening impact would take your breath away. If you saw or heard it coming, you would try and get to a piece of cover and face away from it so as not to catch any shrapnel or secondary debris in the face or eyes. This could be a show-stopper and put you out of action. As we continued to push forward, we caught movement to our right.

Looking across the street to our right, two Somali gunmen were running across an intersecting alley from left to right about 25 yards away. A ranger was laying on his belly, behind a small foot high knoll of dirt at the base of the alley, occasionally grinding his head from left to right, as if to get better protection for his face from the flying bullets, dirt and dust.

Tony screamed at me, "tell him to shoot the mother-fuckers," and I immediately raised my rifle from the low ready, shooting about three feet over the back of the ranger. I tracked the second guy and popped him twice and then transitioned to the first guy and hit him once. The first guy started to crumble and the second guy began trying to push him out of the way into the direction of travel. I immediately screamed at the soldier, "Shoot the mother-fuckers." Due to the noise and gunfire, I doubt if he heard me.

This whole action took about 10 seconds and we turned our attention to our front and continued our movement. We hit the next major intersection with our cover drill and began to move forward down the next street, which was gradually sloping downhill. I remember looking across the street and seeing Norm and his team in the dirt, glancing sideways at us in amazement. A gunman had the angle on them from a two-story building about two blocks away and was tuning them up. This is how combat was. One spot will be safe and 20 feet away your buddies are getting chewed up from an angle that you cannot effectively put fire on.

As we continued forward, halfway down that street on the left side, we could see rangers in a position to our front, huddled around a car under a big leafy tree. As we approached it, we looked to the right and saw the crashed Hawk, upside down in the alley, tail facing us. Without hesitation or guidance, Tony and Scott immediately moved across the alley to our front and began reorienting the rangers and their fire. Fire coming from the alley to the left was heavy and getting worse. You could see the rounds skipping off the far wall as they impacted and continued their journey toward the down aircraft and it's defenders.

I figured we were going to be there for a while and needed to get the force off the street and make ourselves a home. We needed to start expanding our hasty perimeter. I started pushing on a heavy metal gate on the left side of the street, just short of the alley. It did not want to give. I called for my breacher and after one or two seconds, I had a thought flash into my head and told him to disregard. Looking at the gate and the immediate area, it would need a heavy explosive charge and there was nowhere to go to get away from the blast and shock wave. We would probably induce a casualty or two with a charge this big. It was now getting crowded there and I figured I would give it one more try with the shoulder. I was joined by an Air Force CCT attachment, who started shouldering the left side of the gate while I pushed on the right. His side broke first and we were in. The gate opened into a courtyard that would later serve as our command post and casualty collection point. We did a hasty clear of the courtyard and found what appeared to be the front door to our right. I told my Air Force comrade to follow me as I cleared the four-room house. Little did I know that Pete and his team had pulled my Air Force battle buddy out of our two-person stack. I entered a short central hallway and hastily cleared to my left and right. I pied the next room to my left and caught movement. With my non-firing hand, I motioned for the family to come out to me. They were huddled down in the back of the room. Cautiously, they came out toward me. I scanned them and they appeared to be a simple Somali family that happened to be home when we decided to use their house as a firing platform and future Command Post (CP). We secured them and placed them in an interior room of the house, safe and away from outside walls that were subject to rifle and RPG fire. I never saw them after that and assumed they stayed there the entire night.

## AFTER ACTION COMMENTS

### Sustain:

- Ensure worse case movement scenarios are practiced and rehearsed.
- Team leaders control teams to ensure a fluid movement is achieved.
- Avoid rigid movement formations.

**Improve:**
- When using combined forces, require all assets to practice movement techniques as a group and not individual elements.
- Ensure medical procedures address casualty movement, treatment and priority of care.

## WHY LEAD?

Albert Einstein was quoted in the New York Times as saying:

"Only a life lived for others is the life worth while."

Each of us needs to find in ourselves that spark that drives us and ensure it is for honorable reasons. For without that belief and spark, the stress and chaos of combat will strip away the shallow armor of the self-serving leader and ensure their failure. The stronger the belief, the stronger the leader. In today's society, individuals seek leadership positions to enhance their social status, gain power or to simply please the desires of their parents. These reasons are insufficient to sustain the leader when the bullets are thick and soldiers are dying. One must truly believe in their cause and their fellow man to help ensure their survival.

"Until the millennium arrives and countries cease trying to enslave others, it will be necessary to accept one's responsibilities and to be willing to make sacrifices for one's country-as my comrades did. As the troops used to say, "If the country is good enough to live in, it's good enough to fight for." With privilege goes responsibility."

E.B. Sledge

Believe in your cause. The stronger your belief, the stronger your motivation and perseverance will be. You must know it in your heart that it is a worthwhile cause and that you are fighting the good fight. Whether it is the need to contribute or the belief in a greater good, for your buddy, for the team or for your country, find a reason that keeps your fire burning. You will need this fire when the times get tough.

It will help get you through when you are physically exhausted and mentally broken and you can only see far enough to take the next step.

On a personal note, I was rejected from the Army when I was eighteen years old because I told them that I had asthma. I did not let that stop me. I worked for a short time in my second love, law enforcement. Longing for a career in the military, I had a local recruiter check the Army database and see if my name still came up. It did not and I enlisted, this time being a bit wiser on the question of asthma. Probably just seasonal allergies I thought as I marked "No" to the question.

I was fortunate to have a strength, stubbornness and determination that allowed me to fight through or around the system. I knew deep down that I could do anything I put my mind to and that I would not allow minor setbacks or non-applicable administrative rules to chart my life. I refused to live at someone else's expense or choice or worse, indifference. There are two things in life that one cannot control, where you were born and who your parents are. Everything else, we have influence over. Each of us has the ability to chart our own course. What plays an important part is how much sacrifice and hard work you are willing to do to get there. Most are not willing to go the distance and settle for what they are dealt in life. Some have physical or mental handicaps and I have compassion for these folks, but not pity. I remember one of our guys getting his leg blown off during combat operations and he continued to serve for years in the Army. He had a leg for running, swimming, walking and could down hill ski better than anybody I knew. He was dealt a setback, but attacked life and continued to serve as an exceptional soldier. He had an incredible attitude that focused on the goal and not the minor obstacles in the path. This minor setback might slow, but not stop him.

I have also had the honor of serving with individuals in my life who trained and inspired me to levels of excellence that I never imagined. Currently our society tends to churn out individuals that tend to ask the system, "What are you going give or do for me?" We see this attitude all around us. Self-serving individuals concerned with their personal comfort and welfare beyond the norm. These individuals expect the system to take care of them at all costs. When I run across one of these individuals, it makes me want to puke. This attitude is damn near a form of communism.

I was fortunate to serve with men who wanted to know what you could contribute to your country and the team. You were forced to look deep and they looked even deeper. You became accustomed to asking yourself everyday, "what have I done to help the team or our country today?" It was a weight we carried daily. "Max," A.K.A CSM Maxim, would routinely give a short speech oozing with so much heart and emotion that it left you awestruck. He would put into words what you had to feel and believe in to be there. Wrapping ethic, integrity, honor, candor, and duty into a short lecture; it would make you forget about your minor discomfort and feel like a small, but important part of a machine that served a greater good, a "National Asset," as he would refer to the unit.

Failure was not an option during my time in special operations. You took on a mindset of mission accomplishment at all costs. Our equipment is the best that money could buy. Our support personnel and their equipment are on the cutting edge. If something is to fail, it would be the human spirit. We would continually push, hone, sharpen and test ourselves because we knew what was at stake. The survival of our country, our families and each other rested on our ability to penetrate harm's way on demand and accomplish the required mission and return to do it again.

I learned early on that giving your best one time was not good enough. You needed to be consistently good. I would not care to go to combat with an individual that was not consistent, good one day and not the next. I prefer ninety percenters who you could count on the majority of the time. Yes, occasionally you have a bad day, but for the most part, you achieved your goals. If you failed a particular task, you would rehearse it until you got it right. This is what in my mind separates the average or mediocre from the successful. One-time wonders, those who could do it once and not "on demand" would fall by the wayside. The mindset required a hunger for perfection or at least, near-perfection. Occasionally you will find a natural. Most often you would find an individual who had developed a personal system in his life that was proactive and mentally prepared him to do the job.

# ATTAINING COMBAT EFFICIENCY

I firmly believe that we had the right people at the right time with the right training and combat mindset instilled to ensure our success in previously mentioned operations. I have read several arm-chair quarterback versions that describe the mission as a failure or debacle. I disagree. At the operator level, we went in with our heads up, eyes open, lightly armed and punched through the best the enemy had. We stayed as long as we needed against overwhelming odds and accomplishing all missions that day. First, we secured our intended target in a rapid and efficient manner capturing everyone alive. When a Black Hawk helicopter was shot down, we moved on foot through heavy fire and secured it until we were able to recover our comrade's bodies that were trapped in the wreckage. While waiting, we turned the area into a meat-grinder, killing all hostiles that attempted to enter our perimeter. When we did decide to move, we brought all our dead and wounded with us and were ready to fight again hours after this 14 hour battle. Enough said, you get the point.

Politicians and military leaders will continue to put our forces in dangerous situations and it is up to the individual and team to ensure their own survival. How do we prepare ourselves for this type of intense and fast moving action? It begins with selecting individuals who have accepted responsibility for their lives and walk the walk as a performer in the arena.

You must learn to influence yourself before you can influence others. Leadership has been said to be the influencing of others to accomplish a mission. Before you can become a leader, you must first learn to influence and master the physical, emotional, technical and if you will, the spiritual side of yourself. Your personal system should be a simple, efficient and streamlined process to get you to your goal with some time to spare. You see, life is time and time is moving. We can't stop it, but we can learn to use, manage and live with it. When aspiring to be a leader, you must first aspire to be a follower, to do the best job at each level you find yourself, before you set your sights too high, too quickly. Failure to manage your own life will only result in a failure to manage others. Leadership requires time management and efficiency, a system that starts with you. We must move forward on a direct and positive course. Without this course, we will either lose forward momentum or veer off and possibly end up somewhere you were not expecting.

Special Operation's selection is a young man's game requiring physical and mental stamina. Whether the selection process is geared toward the individual or the team player, one must be in the "zone," so to speak, to be successful. You must be physically and mentally right and should be injury free or not nursing an injury. Silly injuries in life can stop your career before it gets started.

## ACCEPT RESPONSIBILITY FOR YOUR LIFE

Subject: Points from *"Dumbing Down Our Kids: Why American Children Feel Good About Themselves But Can't Read, Write or Add,"* by Charles J. Sykes

He talks about how feel-good, politically correct teaching created a generation of kids with no concept of reality and how this concept set them up for failure in the real world.

Rule No. 1: Life is not fair. Get used to it. The average teenager uses the phrase "It's not fair" 8.6 times a day. You got it from your parents, who said it so often you decided they must be the most idealistic generation ever. When they started hearing it from their own kids, they realized Rule No. 1.

Rule No. 2: The real world won't care as much about your self-esteem as much as your school does. It'll expect you to accomplish something before you feel good about yourself. This may come as a shock. Usually, when inflated self-esteem meets reality, kids complain that it's not fair. (See Rule No. 1)

Rule No. 3: Sorry, you won't make $40,000 a year right out of high school. And you won't be a vice president or have a car phone either. You may even have to wear a uniform that doesn't have a Gap label.

Rule No. 4: If you think your teacher is tough, wait 'til you get a boss. He doesn't have tenure, so he tends to be a bit edgier. When you screw up, he's not going to ask you how you feel about it.

Rule No. 5: Flipping burgers is not beneath your dignity. Your grandparents had a different word for burger flipping. They called it opportunity. They weren't embarrassed making minimum wage either.

They would have been embarrassed to sit around talking about Kurt Cobain all weekend.

Rule No. 6: It's not your parents' fault. If you screw up, you are responsible. This is the flip side of "It's my life," and "You're not the boss of me," and other eloquent proclamations of your generation. When you turn 18, it's on your dime. Don't whine about it, or you'll sound like a baby boomer.

Rule No. 7: Before you were born your parents weren't as boring as they are now. They got that way paying your bills, cleaning up your room and listening to you tell them how idealistic you are. And by the way, before you save the rain forest from the blood-sucking parasites of your parents' generation, try delousing the closet in your bedroom.

Rule No. 8: Your school may have done away with winners and losers. Life hasn't. In some schools, they'll give you as many times as you want to get the right answer. Failing grades have been abolished and class valedictorians scrapped, lest anyone's feelings be hurt. Effort is as important as results. This, of course, bears not the slightest resemblance to anything in real life. (See Rule No. 1, Rule No. 2 and Rule No. 4.)

Rule No. 9: Life is not divided into semesters, and you don't get summers off. Not even Easter break. They expect you to show up every day. For eight hours. And you don't get a new life every 10 weeks. It just goes on and on. While we're at it, very few jobs are interested in fostering your self-expression or helping you find yourself. Fewer still lead to self-realization. (See Rule No. 1 and Rule No. 2.)

Rule No. 10: Television is not real life. Your life is not a sitcom. Your problems will not all be solved in 30 minutes, minus time for commercials. In real life, people actually have to leave the coffee shop to go to jobs. Your friends will not be as perky or pliable as Jennifer Aniston.

Rule No. 11: Be nice to nerds. You may end up working for them. We all could.

Rule No. 12: Smoking does not make you look cool. It makes you look moronic. Next time you're out cruising, watch an 11-year-old with a butt in his mouth. That's what you look like to anyone over 20. Ditto for "expressing yourself" with purple hair and/or pierced body parts.

Rule No. 13: You are not immortal. (See Rule No. 12.) If you are under the impression that living fast, dying young and leaving a beautiful corpse is romantic, you obviously haven't seen one of your peers at room temperature lately.

Rule No. 14: Enjoy this while you can. Sure parents are a pain, school's a bother, and life is depressing. But someday you'll realize how wonderful it was to be a kid. Maybe you should start now. You're welcome.

Realize right now, that you are the only one in control of your life. If you choose to make change, excel or just be happy, it is ultimately up to you. You must believe this and put it into action to make it happen. Too many times individuals quit before they get started by blaming others for their misfortune. I can't do this because...... They blame others for an accident, not getting promoted and a host of other self-perceived problems. The bottom line, don't sell yourself short on your ability to change your own world.

Life is like a compass or orienteering course. You can move fast and get somewhere, but it may not be where you intended. The skilled navigator will study their map, look at the terrain and choose between the fast and slow routes and determine which is best for their journey. Many times in difficult terrain, it is wise to pick out check-points to ensure you're on the right track. Life is the same way. Occasionally you need to pick your head up and look around and see where you are and if you are making progress you expected. While navigating a multi-kilometer leg of a compass course in the Northeast, I had the choice of running the ridges, going up and down through generally light brush with a narrow footpath to guide me or to get down next to the creek and hope the brush was not too thick and that I might find a small game trail. After a bit of up and down on the ridge route, I said to myself "to hell with this," and dropped into the valley below, finding not a game trail, but a level super highway size road that paralleled the creek and took me smoothly to my next check point.

Sometimes you just need to look around and see what progress you're making for the effort your putting out. Focusing on the terrain ten feet in front of you and day dreaming at the wrong time will cause you to sometime take the hard path and even overshoot a checkpoint. Worse case, you might veer off course, you may end up somewhere you did not intend and you might not be able to get back to the intended destination. On the land navigation course, it will cost you time, mental and physical energy to get back. In life, it might not allow you to fulfill your dreams due to age, a family commitment, or something of this nature.

## PERSONAL EFFORT

An old friend told me that life is like the saying on a soda machine, "NO DEPOSIT, NO RETURN." I have found this to be simple and true. Today's society tends to produce a person who requires instantaneous feedback, rewards or results with minimal input on their part. I have found that most rewards or accomplishments are not easily won or earned. We get out of life what we put into it.

In the physical arena, it generally takes 2000-3000 repetitions for muscle memory to refine or instill a desired movement or action. Some remember the old saying of "practice makes perfect," but the reality is that you must focus on every move to ensure that you're doing it correctly. "Perfect practice makes perfect." The next question you need to ask is, " Have you met your standard or society's standard today?

Society has become "kinder-gentler," in their effort not to hurt one's feelings or make them feel inadequate when developing standards. Most standards, whether it be the military or the average police department are set low to accommodate the bottom feeders of life who lack the personal pride, motivation or determination to rise above the rest. Routinely, we put military personnel and law enforcement officers into harm's way, with less proficiency in the use of their firearms and in worse physical shape, than the hostile elements they are going to encounter. A recent example of this is the Federal Sky Marshals and their shooting program and standards. Initially, it was a top-notch program upholding the highest shooting standards. Since the influx of thousands of new Sky Marshals into the program, the standards have been drastically cut. The designers of the initial standards knew the dangers of making a surgical shot on a "tubular target," such as an airplane. They knew that accurate and rapid shots were needed to neutralize threats, some possibly running down the aisle toward the folks driving the bird. You would not want an officer to miss and send rounds into the cockpit. This could be a show-stopper for everyone on board.

As an individual skill, I will use shooting as a simple example. Shooting is a perishable skill and what I consider a personal skill. I should not have a Team Leader hovering over me to ensure I dry fire and practice. I should dry-fire on my own, two to three times a week because it is the right thing to do. Dry fire will ensure that I make a surgical shot with minimal rounds fired, killing the bad guy. It will help me to keep all my rounds in my desired target and possibly not allow the threat to kill one of my comrades or innocent people.

During dry fire or "dry practice," as some describe it, you go through all the mechanics of shooting from your ready position to punching the gun out in an efficient manner, aligning the sights and then dropping the hammer without disturbing the sights. The standards I practice are mostly fired at seven yards and you have to hit the kill zone in one second or less from a high-ready position. So, when I practice, I practice at not one second, but at .90 seconds by using a standard shot timer that alerts you when to shoot and generates a second beep at the desired time limit. By practicing to be faster, I am not just trying to "meet" the standard, I am trying to exceed it.

## BE SIMPLE AND EFFICIENT AND COMPETE WITH YOURSELF FIRST

Keep our life as simple and efficient as possible. How? Learn with each stumble or failure. Failure is only an opportunity to excel. The perception in which your mind chooses to visualize your challenges in life will enable your successes or enhance your failures. Learn not to worry, but to channelize worry, anxiety, or dread into positive action that will enable you to succeed.

Set your goals and determine the best course for achieving them. Go back to the land navigation analogy. Find useful vehicles that can help you achieve your goals and this may include important factors such as time and money. Airline pilots are a prime example. Many use the military as a stepping-stone to their dreams of becoming an airline pilot. They allow the Army, Navy or Air Force to pay for all that expensive flight training and hours. They use the largest aviation organizations in the world to support their learning while also serving their country. It is not only smart, but efficient.

Another simple example is that of succeeding on an Army physical fitness test. Most people dread it and fail to adequately prepare. Many will only run two miles to get ready for a two-mile test. Minimums. We have become a society that strives for the minimum standard and this is how we live our lives. Failure to put in the desired time and effort will reward you with only middle of the road performance. Once in a while you will find one natural in the crowd, not often, but occasionally. For the rest of us who have to struggle to succeed, I would not have it any other way. I find reward and satisfaction in working hard for something and attaining even a small goal.

But, back to the preparation for the physical training test. How could you more adequately prepare for a physical training test? First, get with someone who is successful and ask them their secrets. Most often they are likely to tell you that you have to pay your dues by hard work and training. Making the time to train might be the key. You might have to sacrifice sleep and get up early to get workouts in.

Doing more to prepare, versus less, will always help you. Set target goals and dates for your training. Use these as check points on your personal map to see if you're heading in the right direction. Get up early on the day of the test and get warmed up by doing a warm up run and exercise. Get the blood flowing and get your muscles right. Too many individuals are still tired and tight from sleeping and their muscles are now warmed up enough to get them efficiently through the event.

Moreover, as an instructor, I see many students not taking the time to develop their own personal system and instead watching the other individual. Too many times we look at others with envy for a perceived talent or skill and fail to see the hard work and sacrifice they put toward their success. Two simple examples that come to mind are shooting (technical skill) and physical training. Accurate and rapid shooting requires that you proceed deliberately and master the basics or fundamentals first. Developing muscle memory by repetition is the key. Generally 2000-3000 reps will get you on your way to subconsciously mastering the skill. You can watch someone else and evaluate their technique, but don't become engrossed in it. Find out what works for you and your body.

Too many times the general principles will work for mastering the gun, but fine tuning the individual quirks are just as important as it is to break through a speed or accuracy barrier to reach a higher level of performance.

Physically, train at your own speed and level of condition. Draw and mental curtain to block out useless information and focus on what is best for you. If you try and go too fast, you have the increased chance of getting hurt and then you waste a great deal of time in rehab and you lose valuable time moving toward your goal. In addition, your strengths and weaknesses are different than someone else. You must target your training to your individual needs.

Don't be afraid to video yourself and use it to critique the real you. We routinely have a "perception" as to what we look like during an action. The video camera will not lie. This is where perception and reality crash together. Once you get past the initial shock we all go through of what you look like, you can then methodically break down your actions and figure out positive solutions to problems. You learn to accept the visual as what it is, real time, real truth.

## GET OUT OF YOUR COMFORT ZONE AND DEVELOP MENTAL TOUGHNESS

At the individual level, you need to get out of your comfort zone and push your limits. Too many times we fail to break out and change or experience the positive aspects of change. I have found that for a great deal of people, human nature is to seek the status quo. The military and the government usually set the bar low to accommodate the current social status quo. Whether to appease a social group or risk hurt feelings or just make waves in the EO arena, we lower the overall strength and capability of our group when we lower the standards.

I use the dreaded military road march to illustrate a way of pushing through those walls of discomfort that we routinely hit in life. These are the walls that we need to go over or around to attain personal goals or objectives. Most individuals who have served in our armed forces can remember the pain of a road march. For infantry units, the road march is near and dear to their hearts. This reflection of the road march was sent to me and it goes as follows:

A) It allows you to challenge your soul.
B) It teaches you the importance of teamwork.
C) It provides a mirror reflecting who you are.
D) It exposes all good and bad in yourself.

D)  There's no way to hide on a road march.
E)  It strengthens trust in your leaders.
F)  It toughens you mentally.
G)  It beats complaining right out of you.
H)  It orients you to authority.
I)  It makes you think about others.
J)  It matures you.
K)  It makes you more objective.
L)  It provides a frame of reference for suffering.

> The Road March is the crucible in which the soul is
> refined. Pulling a trigger is easy. Humping the load
> over the distance is where you find out who will be
> on the ambush site to pull the trigger with you. The
> Road March defines you. Never quit. Come in
> ugly if you have to, but come in.

The road march is a level playing field that can enhance your physical and mental skills and endurance. The distance does not change for any race, age or gender. The weight you carry and move from point A to B is the same for everyone. The variable in the equation is your mindset, heart and physical condition. The casual observer will look at a road march as a simple event, not requiring much time or preparation. This is far from reality.

Important factors that ensure success for this event are your mental and physical planning, preparation and attention to detail. Failure to properly condition your boots and your feet are the quickest tickets to failure. Proper training tells you how to buy and size proper fitting boots. You learn to rotate your boots during training, breaking them in evenly. You learn to keep your toenails trimmed or you will lose them through continual pounding and pressure on the front of your boot. Soaking your feet in Epson salts several times a week will dry and toughen your feet. You choose socks that provide cushion and protection and discard worn ones. You pad your rucksack so that after three to four hours of constant wear, it has not punched a bleeding hole in your body that you can feel with every step. Your training regimen is another learning point, starting with short distances carrying a light weight load is the key to foot and physical conditioning. Starting with far unrealistic distances and heavy weight is the quickest way to incur an injury. You will only find torn up feet, joints, back pain and sores with going too heavy too fast. All these points and we also need to mention your personal water intake. Not hydrating prior to the march, can cause you to fail. Dressing too warm will cause you to overheat and collapse.

Once you start the march you are going to hit a wall of discomfort. You need to know the difference between discomfort and pain and when to stop. If you condition yourself to stop when feeling discomfort and not pain, you're setting yourself up for failure. You're not only training your body to stop, but more importantly, it trains your mind to give in.

You need to plan, prepare, rehearse and make it happen and do this cycle over and over again. By properly planning and rehearsing, you take away all the excuses and realize that you have all that is necessary to succeed or fail. Many Americans are weak minded people who love excuses. As we used to say, the maximum effective range of an excuse is zero meters. You either succeeded or failed. Period. Find a physical challenge that requires two-three hours of mental endurance to be successful. You could start with a long walk and then add weight. It could be a bike ride or even a run. Whatever you decide to do, it will strengthen your mind, body and spirit to a higher plane.

## TRADITIONAL AND UNTRADITIONAL APPROACHES TO ACHIEVING LEADERSHIP GOALS

Routinely we migrate through the process of life, from elementary and high school to college and then a job. This route provides the standard middle-of-the road approach to learning and leadership. We may punch all the right tickets, but something is lost. That something is heart. Many individuals that I have watched endure this process don't have the internal fire, the killer drive or instinct for leadership. They are comfortable with status quo "management" instead of leadership, and don't want to rock the boat with anything outside the proverbial box.

Traditional education does not usually promote aggressive and innovative leaders, but produces a rather a limited leader with a limited heart. It encourages students to **rise to** a standard that the system deems good or bad, but is generally **geared** toward the masses and the status quo. Generally, our system **lacks** mechanisms for identifying those best suited for leadership and providing them a route to their goals and dreams. Sometimes leaders don't **know** what they don't know. Others simply don't understand what it **takes** and they must be enlightened to fully understand that they can **have** an impact on those being led.

First, I didn't go into life **wanting** to be a leader. This may sound counterproductive. As I gained **experience**, I learned that I must have an attitude of trying to do the **best** job at the task at hand instead of constantly wanting to be **promoted** or aspiring to be a leader. I found that leadership challenges will **eventually** come. Some uninformed parents have the most problem with this idea. They feel that their little Johnny would make a natural leader. Most parents have not been around great leaders and would not know a good leader if they were smacked by one.

I suggest that students start by jotting down the good and bad points of leaders they respect and detest and use them as lessons or guidelines in their leadership challenges. Mark down arrogance, excessive pride, laziness as key bad or counterproductive points to be avoided. Leave your ego behind on this journey and ratchet up the personal controlled aggressiveness. You can be aggressive and still be polite. You can be well mannered and not piss off or be a threat to those above, below or on your level.

## THE JOURNEY OR THE DESTINATION?

What is more important to you? This may help answer the question of why you're doing what you do. Is it for prestige, fame, notoriety? Or is it to help your fellow man who is trying to make it through the same life, bombarded by the same struggles and challenges, trying to take one day at a time.

I have come to the conclusion that "Life is a work in progress, take one day at a time and enjoy each step, whether painful or delightful." When life gets tough and it looks like the gators are going to get you, step back, take a deep breath and start killing them one at a time, usually the closest one first.

During your journey and challenges, you will need to keep your integrity intact. A Special Operations friend named Oz relayed a story of integrity and values to me. He said that life is like climbing a slow gradual hill with a rucksack full of bricks. The bricks represent integrity and values. As the hill tires you, some tend to drop a brick here and there to lighten their load. Many find that through the process, they reach the top of the hill with an empty rucksack. Some though, keep all their bricks through the journey. Some who don't have all the bricks at the beginning of the journey pick one up here and there along their way. You may find that some steps might be unpleasant, but enjoy them all and try and pick a few bricks up along the way. Find that balance during your "movement" through life. Compare life to a navigation course and plan where you want to go and how you're going to get there. Don't be afraid to take an unorthodox path to get to your destination.

## KEY POINTS

- Establish Your Personal Reasons For Becoming A Leader And Ensure That You Are Willing To Travel The Path To Reach Your Goal.
- Compete With Yourself First And Don't Worry About Others. Tailor Your Training Program To Your Specific Strengths And Weaknesses.
- Get Out Of Your Comfort Zone And Develop A Mental Toughness To Help You Weather The Hard Times.
- Enjoy The Journey As The Destination Is Often Too Short A Visit.

# CHAPTER FOUR

# SELECTION

*"Selection is a never ending process"*

(An old Special Ops Saying)

- SELECTION TARGET = CONSISTENT LEADERS WHO MAINTAIN THE STANDARD, BUT PREFER TO EXCEED IT
- INITIAL SELECTION FOCUS – TEAM PLAYER VS. STRONG INDIVIDUAL
- INDIVIDUAL REALISTIC TESTS AND EVALUATIONS
- MENTAL PREPARATION
- PHYSICAL PREPARATION
- LONG TERM/ON GOING SELECTION FOCUS
- SETTING UP A SELECTION PROCESS
- SAMPLE GUT CHECKS

## AK

We got the word from an "unreliable" informant that there was a high level meeting taking place at the target designated AK and that there was a possibility of the top dog being there. Putting eyes on the target, we saw that there were guards present outside the building, which was a good indicator that something was amiss. The team leaders reported to the tactical operations center (TOC) and began their planning session. The target consisted of seven to eight neatly rowed apartment buildings, occasionally separated by a small house or building between them with an average of 50 yards of space between the structures. Our pinpoint target was a small house in between the third and fourth buildings. I thought it should not be too hard to find, but drew a sketch map just to be safe. I stuffed it into my vest where my "chicken plate" normally goes. A chicken plate is ceramic plate and the part of a vest that actually stops rifle bullets. The plates are heavy and bulky and I normally did not wear one on operations where mobility was a concern. I would rather be fast and agile like a jungle cat than slow and easy to hit like a tank.

We planned the hit and moved to the birds with the pilots for our final briefing. The flight went well and we were inbound when the gun birds gave the guard force an education in firepower about 30 seconds before we landed. I watched as the tracers impacted their target area and bounced up off the building into the sky. Our ride was smooth and we were supposed to land directly adjacent to the target building. On our approach, Kim serviced the guard shack with a 40mm round just to keep any potential occupants honest. As with most missions, nothing is perfect and our pilot's sharp eyes saved us again from running into a single power line that ran across the street in our landing spot. We landed long and off our mark. We moved straight to a low wall that surrounded the compound and started looking for our target building. At night, under NVG's (Night Vision Goggles), looking down the row of buildings, it was difficult to see which one was one, two, three, etc. I was looking for a structure of sorts and I could not pinpoint it. We headed toward the first building and linked up with a sister team and started clearing apartments. They went downstairs and we moved upstairs, leap-frogging with our security element. We charged the first door and began our clearing. The rooms were sparse, some furniture in the living rooms, maybe a bed and upright closet in the bedrooms. We found a door that was locked and I told Scott to charge it. As he did, a woman in the apartment came to me with a key and I told here we did not need it. He called burning and we took cover and with a blast, the door was open. We cleared it and found a "case" of local currency. It was only about one-hundred dollars, U.S. We left it and went outside, linking up with our sister team on the end of our apartment building. I pulled my sketch map out of my vest pouch and looked it over. We were one to two buildings too far down. We moved down and spotted a house in between two of the large apartment buildings. As we moved to it, we saw other teams ready to penetrate it and joined them. They breached and we entered behind them and began to flow through the target. Teams became mixed and we would reorganize in rooms deeper in the structure. Distraction devices were thrown and their detonation would send up a dust cloud in the structure of all the filth and dirt that was on the floors. Within one to two breaths, the back of your throat was coated with a fine nasty tasting dust that had settled on the floors and walls of the structure.

We kept clearing and while I was following my partner into one room, a child that appeared to be about six years old tried to run out past us and ran square into the magazine of my weapon. The sharp corner left a small gash in his forehead and he ran crying back to his parents holding his wound. This room contained a heap of junk and debris that we had to move on and around. The next room we cleared contained a pile of junk covered by an old nasty cloth tarp. My partner covered while I yanked the tarp away, leaving rats scrambling around the mess. "Delightful," I thought to myself.... This portion of the structure was clear.

We moved outside and found a door to another part of the building. Breaching it led us through a kitchen and to a dead end pantry. It was clear. Prior to the pantry on the left was a half bookcase up against a wall with a full-length curtain behind it. Pulling the bookcase away, we found a door behind the curtain. With a quick pull, the curtain came off as did the entire door. We entered the room and found a family lined up, facing our entry point. The kids were one end, the father on the other and the father was holding out an infant as a shield. I moved and cleared left and we secured the scene. I became pissed and told the boys to take all males over 16 years of age, flex tie them and we would take them back to the rear, to include the brave father who used his infant as a shield.

Outside we linked up with another team leader who requested two of my guys for additional clearing duties. I assigned two of my men to him and told them where to link back up with me. We cleared a couple more doors in the immediate area, established security and consolidated our prisoners. Waiting for my guys, the commander got a report of another house-type structure at the far end of the apartment complex. My men returned and we headed for the new target with a sister team. We passed through a security position and I let them know where I was going and that I was going to come back through them. As we approached the target building we found that we were hitting it from the rear. I dropped off at a back gate and the other teams moved to the front. My breacher put a hefty charge on the center of the metal gate, where the two swinging sides joined. He called burning and we took cover on both sides, out of the blast radius. A few seconds later, the charge went off with a large boom. We moved through the smoke and I caught movement and a screaming and crying off to my right. Shining my gun light, I found a goat on the ground, quivering, doing the kicking chicken. As best I could tell, the goat was a pet of sorts and came up to and sniffed the back of the gate opposite the charge. You can probably guess what happened next. The charge went off and blew the goats, ass over tea kettle into the dirt. We moved past the four legged casualty and moved to the back door of the residence. The door was recessed in an alcove and we charged it. Another heavy charge was placed, so I tucked into a corner a few feet away and watched as fiery debris flew past me. Looking at the breach point, the homeowners had placed a dresser up against the door to block our entry. The dresser was now three to four inches tall and spread out down the hallway. We entered and caught sight of our sister team down the hall. We cleared to them and joined them on the final room. As before, we entered and the father had the family lined up in front of our entry point, holding out his infant as a shield. I thought to myself, "what a cowardly low-life mother fucker." I told the boys to secure him up and that he would be going for a helicopter ride.

We took our prisoner and began to move back to our first target building. We passed through our security position without incident and headed for the link-up. We deposited our prisoner with the prisoner handling teams and got the exfiltration order from the boss. It turns out the two knuckle-heads that used the infants as shields were high ranking officers in bad guy's militia.

# AFTER ACTION COMMENTS

### Sustain:

- Be prepared to land off target and know the immediate and surrounding area.
- Have maps ready and available for all personnel.
- Keep discrimination rules simple and to a high standard.

### Improve:

- Think about dust respirators in nasty environments.

# SELECTION TARGET = CONSISTENT LEADERS WHO MAINTAIN THE STANDARD, BUT PREFER TO EXCEED IT

The first order of business when structuring the selection process is choosing a safe and fair system that is geared toward the mission/job criteria or towards the individual's ability to learn the job. Having discussed the individual traits that one should strive to develop in their lives in chapter one, we need to now look at the individual we wish to select as a leader. Should all leaders be volunteers or should you determine who goes through the selection process? Does their immediate supervisor need to recommend them for the selection process? These questions boil down to the issue of filling your selection process. Success is generally found in individuals that wish to voluntarily participate in the selection process because they have the drive and desire to do so. Occasionally, you will have to urge someone who has become too settled in their "comfort zone" and realize they have found a "nitch" and enjoy the comfortable life. This type of person who needs encouragement or urging on is generally an individual who lacks self-confidence. While I don't believe that someone should develop their self-confidence at the expense of others, I feel that every so often you can see the potential in someone and all they need is the right counseling and encouragement to spark a desire to expand their potential. In the end, all you need is to show them the door and allow them the opportunity to walk through.

# INITIAL SELECTION FOCUS –
## TEAM PLAYER VS. INDIVIDUAL

The selection focus, or should I say the individual focus is next. It is important to first understand that some team players will not do well without the team surrounding them for support. Some selection processes are geared specifically to the team concept and understand that they may have a weak individual and the team may help them make it through the selection process. Generally not as strong or initiative oriented as the individual selection process, the group selection process will allow individuals to season, learn and mature within the group, should they choose to, and the "group" will aid them in passing the selection process.

The individual process on the other hand is looking for a resourceful individual that can work for extended periods without contact and can muster the drive and self- initiative from within and does not need the security of the group to succeed. The structure of your selection process can be tailored to each of these individuals.

The individual selection process can be geared toward individual initiative and drive with challenges pitting individuals against individuals or time. Time might be one of the criteria in the selection process. How do we establish a time standard for an individual? Several ways exist, but one simple method is to have a group who has already passed the selection process run the event "cold" for time and then add all the times together and divide it by the numbers in the group. You can then add 10-20% to the time to compensate for the experience level of the group and you now have a standard. This can be done for land navigation movements, shooting courses or typing tests. It simply does not matter.

The group test can be accomplished the same way, by taking a group and having them run or "validate" the drill, taking the average times and adding 10-20 percent. Then with this new 10-20 percent standard, have the entire group run it again and see how they stack up against the new standard.

# INDIVIDUAL REALISTIC TESTS AND EVALUATIONS

Special Forces employ a team concept for selection, but also challenges the soldier at the individual level.  Land navigation is one medium that equally discriminates against all players and provides a level playing field for candidates.  In navigation courses, the ground does not change nor do the distances.  The weight and equipment are the same for all.  The ability to think and properly select routes is one variable that students can practice and become proficient, in an effort to minimize route selection mistakes.  How does one get better at land navigation?  By simply taking initiative and practicing walks on their own time.  I know countless soldiers that spend their weekends with a map, compass and rucksack, practicing navigating cross-country and on roads.  While navigating, they developed their strength and endurance as well as their mental preparation.

One will also learn common mistakes made in land navigation, such as not walking far enough. You see, as you walk, you become fatigued. Your pace will shorten and you will not travel as fast or as far.  You fatigue and your brain will say to your body that you should be there by now and you are actually short of your target.  Generally the unskilled navigator will not trust the checkpoints they have established on their maps and will stop short and look for the point, wasting valuable time on their route. By getting used to the discomfort of the rucksack and the time it takes to travel at a certain pace, you will strengthen your mind and you body.  Further, this not only shows initiative, but heart.  Read back to the road march quote and it will put it in perspective.  Total focus is required even if you're distracted by "discomfort."

# MENTAL PREPARATION

Mental preparation is a personal thing and as an individual, you will develop your own system of doing business.  Using the land navigation analogy, some individuals will look at it as fun and program routes in areas that will not only challenge them, but will offer them some visual stimulation.  Some might take to the mountains and walk challenging routes and rugged terrain, while others might take to the beach and let the soft sand break down and build up their muscles while watching the surf. Some turn the walk into fun and bring family members. Others see it as a challenge and push themselves to beat time distance goals they have set. Still others see it is a means to attaining a goal and simply "gut out" the walks. If possible, make it a fun and enjoyable ride to your goal. If nothing else, use it as meditation time. I remember going for hours on rucksack marches and the scenery allowed me to clear my mind for hours and come off it physically pumped and mentally energized.

## PHYSICAL PREPARATION

Personal physical preparation is again a personal area where the individual needs to maximize their training time to accomplish two or three things while getting their workout in. The first rule in the beginning of your successful training session is to start slow and light. You want to let your body adjust to the walking you're going to do and it may take several sessions to do this. There are no shortcuts that I have found to walking with a ruck, other than to put it on and hump it. Having said this, select comfortable and cushioned socks and footwear and watch for hot pots. Hot spots will generally start to appear because of soft feet or ill-fitting socks or shoes. The walking process will begin to condition your feet to your weight, while you are conforming your feet to your shoes. It may take several weeks to work the aches, pains and soreness out. I have found that if you start slow, your discomfort will be minimal. An aspirin after the walk will help your body heal. Soaking your feet in warm-to-hot Epson Salts will make your feet feel a great deal better and it will dry and toughen them. If you develop a blister or two, Epson Salts after you march is the hot ticket. It will physically help your feet and mentally it will relax you.

"Too Far, Too Fast" is a recipe for disaster. Too much distance will break down your muscles, your feet and your spirits without a positive return for your time and effort. Too much weight too quickly will tear down your muscles and joints and is the fastest way to end a training program. I have watched countless individuals tear a muscle or blow out a knee by training improperly, causing them a temporary (months) or a severe setback (years or more). Taking care of your body is the key. One knee surgery can take you out of your window of opportunity for a lifetime.

# LONG TERM/ON GOING SELECTION FOCUS

The quote "Selection is a never ending process," is true. A selection process can be structured as a brief "snapshot" of the individual or it can be a longer picture or even a short movie. Still longer, it can be a mini-series or trilogy where it lasts for a year or more. There are selection processes that last over a year, sometimes two, where the candidate is on probation for a period of time. I still consider this part of the selection process.

The importance of the position you are selecting individuals for generally dictate the length of selection process. You can get a snapshot of your candidate through applications and the paper trail they generate, but we all know the inflated paper trails that are being produced that don't accurately reflect the real candidate. I have seen the "school chasers," those individuals who paper their walls with certificates from all the schools they attended, but rarely can they perform. Most of these chasers seek the schools for promotion rather than to bring back the information and make their people or team better. There are those who do have a sincere interest in bettering themselves or the team. Occasionally, they will get a school, but generally, it is few and far between.

These school chasers will have stunning resumes, but are functionally illiterate in their fields and often socially inept. Most of the time they have put so much energy in getting schools, they never do their job or their entire focus is spent on getting the "slot," that they never have a chance to develop their team. Further, if they are always in school, they are never home to pass the knowledge and develop their teams.

I understand if there are time and money constraints in your selection process, but if the job is prone to life and death high stress situations, maybe the selection process should reflect that. With proper selection, you will quickly weed out the paper chasers in short order and will find the individuals with substance and character.

# SETTING UP AND VALIDATING

How do you set-up a selection process? It can be announced or an unannounced, or a "surprise" process that is geared toward their job. It can be made up of one test, several tests or multiple different tests that check several different areas of interest.

For the tactical team member, the selection can be made up of several endurance events that require the individual to think when they become tired or fatigued. It can focus on their individual ability to think in high stress situations and not self-destruct when discomfort and fatigue set in. A twenty four hour test will tell you a great deal about an individual. Calling them in late at night, unannounced and then having them perform several low intensity physical events throughout the night, denying them sleep would be a good start. Then begin the day with stress shooting and practical scenarios. You could end early that day or run it into the night. The bottom line is that the more time, effort, planning and thought that you put into the process, the better candidate you will select. As a general rule, most will become "cranky" with lack of sleep and hopefully will have the professionalism and maturity to control and deal with it. If they do not control their temper and emotions, they will let it out for all to see. This will be a red flag during the selection process that is simple to spot.

How do we see this red flag. Easy. Team Leaders and members should be running the selection process and should be assigned to run or monitor a section or time period of the event. This way, if you use four teams to run your process, you can get four individual assessments of the individuals from four different perspectives. You can even keep the problems from one evaluation team to the next, where the next team to receive them gets a true picture of their attitudes and performance. This technique also spread out the work and allows all the team members to see all the potential candidates and vice versa. Team members walking a road march for example and then conducting a shoot afterwards will have the same team next to them the entire way and one or two members shooting with them to show them the standard. It is up to your imagination on how you set it up.

## SAMPLE GUT CHECK

I used to perform what I termed "Gut Checks" from time to time on ROTC cadets. The date was known for the check and not more else. I originally started the "gut check" to see who would be authorized to wear a black "beret" as part of the Ranger Challenge in ROTC. Since then, former Chief of Staff General Shinseki thought it would be better for everyone to have one as it would increase their self-esteem. Another costly and ineffective fallacy by an ignorant leader who would rather give someone something for nothing to soldiers who have not earned it. Originally worn by U.S. Army Rangers, the Army managers decided to waste a great deal of money by taking the Rangers black beret and giving it to everyone and their brother. Snubbing the Rangers and their heritage, they forced this elite unit to adopt another color beret and now watch and cringe as soldiers in every walk of life, wear their new berets like pizza chefs. Enough venting and back to the story.

For my "gut check," a bulletin would be posted on the board for those wishing to try out, or qualify. The notice would give a date and time where to be, with a prescribed packing list of items that were to be placed in their rucksack. On the day of the event, I would walk in at the precise time and the door would be closed behind me. If you were late, you would wait until the next semester to try out.

I would then give the cadets a mission statement that was brief and limited. They were randomly selected and placed on teams. A team leader was randomly selected and they were given five minutes to brief and ready their team for movement. The course would have been scouted and run several times in the months prior, quietly and discreetly so no one knew the routes, distances, or events except for those administering the event. Five minutes later, we were moving. Generally, it was dark out and we started walking. I liked to walk, to warm them up for greater things to come. I also liked to check the group for injuries as we walked. You could pick out a limp a mile away and quickly pinpoint a potential problem. I would ensure that team leaders would constantly monitor their people for injuries and that they would continue to drink water. We would walk, sometimes for two hours, depending on the pace of the group. I set the pace, but it was my goal for everyone to finish, no matter how slow they were. The slower they walked the longer they carried the weight on their backs. There would be a price to pay for taking their time.

While we walked, the fear of the unknown was the first stress that would settle into their minds. Subtlety they had to deal with it and learn to control it within themselves. Their bodies would begin to ache and after the first hour or so, they would become warmed up to a point that their bodies were ready for more. During one event, we stopped three to four miles into the walk for a break and each cadet picked up a sandbag to load into their rucksack. This played on their minds and body. During the break, team leaders checked to ensure their team members drank water and checked for injuries and then reported back to me. I then personally checked to ensure that they also drank water and asked if they were injured before continuing.

During the movement, if someone fell back more than 100 yards, I had a van following the group that would pick them up. This was a safety precaution and I would have the individual shuttled back or taken to another point to help run the course. We walked with our rucks for another two to three miles and then took another break. Team Leaders were told to have everyone drink water and put their tennis shoes on, placing their boots in their rucks and their rucks on a truck. This took no longer than five to ten minutes and then we were on a group run. The teams stayed together on this run and we began slow and steady. We ran for five miles through the town back to the college to a point where our obstacle course began. The rucks were waiting for us and we got the sand bags out.

Moving as a team, the members had to take their sand bags through the course and they would deposit them at a point that they did not know about. I needed to build a fighting position in the course and this was the easiest way to get the sandbags there. As the teams headed out, their instructions were to put the sand bag down and negotiate the obstacle and then recover the sand bag. The pace was a fast walk, but the team could only travel as fast as their slowest person. Halfway thorough the course, the teams dropped their sandbags in a predesignated spot and they then began a jog on the course. Overall length of the course round trip was one and one-half to two miles. Upon completion of the obstacle course, they were directed to pickup their rucksacks and move to the college stadium. There they took the standard Army Physical Training test consisting of push-ups for two minutes, a break, sit-ups for two minutes and then a break. Finally they did a two-mile run for time. They are then told that I am sorry, the gut check is now over and they return to the classroom where they started.

Cadets learned first hand that "selection is a never ending process." During my time at the ROTC assignment, I ran the gut check or a variation of this event seven or eight times, generally once a semester. I remember students of all shapes and size that were proud of what they accomplished that day. I showed them that they could move 12-13 miles through various unknown physical and mental challenges and still pass an Army PT test. As a matter of fact, most did as well on the test that day as they did when they took it cold.

"When you can do what I do, you can go where I go"

(An old special ops saying)

I think it is important for leaders to have "gut checks" to ensure that the force is meeting a combat standard and not the minimum Army standard. Today the Army has a grading system for their physical training test that would make your head spin. In an effort to "equalize" everyone, it breaks down categories into male and female and then into many age categories. This effort to make everyone feel good is beyond me. There should be one standard for those who are subject to combat conditions, a minimum standard. Why? The last time I checked, a machine gun, its ammo or a 100 meter sprint under fire is not different for a male or female, young or old soldier. Why should a Command Sergeant Major in the Army with over 20 years in have to do less physical training than a private who is going to the same combat theater? Why should a woman who does less on a physical fitness test get a higher score and rating on her yearly evaluation report. It makes no sense. All this inequality does is attempt to make the individual feel better about themselves for doing less. To add, it weakens the capability of the entire force while providing a place for discrimination and dissention to grow.

## KEY POINTS

- DESIGN SELECTION PROCESSES AROUND CURRENT TASKS, LEARNING ABILITIES OR INITIATIVE.
- DEVELOP A LEVEL PLAYING FIELD TO CONDUCT YOUR SELECTION PROCESS WHERE ALL INDIVIDUALS ARE EQUAL. THIS WILL TAKE AWAY EXCUSES BE WEAKER INDIVIDUALS.

# CHAPTER FIVE

# TEAM LEADERSHIP

*Of Every 100 Men:*
*10 Shouldn't Even be Here*
*80 are Nothing but Targets*
*9 Are Real Fighters...*
*....We are Lucky to have them....*
*....They the Battle Make....*
*-"Ah but the one, one of them is a Warrior...*
*...and he will bring the others back."*

Hericletus, 500 years BC

- THE KEY TO CONSISTENT SUCCESS
- TEAM MAKE UP
- TEAM LEADER SELECTION
- TEAM LEADER DUTIES
- THE ADMINISTRATIVE TEAM LEADER
- THE TEAM LEADER AS A TRAINER
- THE TACTICAL TEAM LEADER
- TACTICAL TEAM LEADER TIPS

## THE CALL

It was a quiet Sunday afternoon and the day was passing slowly. Some passed the time with an early morning run or a physical training session. Others read, or did their laundry in mop buckets by the shower point. As the day progressed, we watched as the crowds gathered at the reviewing stand, an area routinely used by the local leadership to give speeches to the local citizens. The reviewing stands and platform were a simple area, consisting of a two-story structure with a platform that had overhead cover from the sun. The platform faced a large street and open area that would support literally thousands of local people who came to hear from their leaders.

Some of these leaders we wanted to talk to. Many were key leaders in the militia who we were having problems with. The problem was getting to them. The back of the grandstand area had several structures adjoining it where the dignitaries vehicles could pull up, deposit their guest and then stage for a quick get away. The other problem was the crowd. Thousands would gather to listen to the leaders speak. During the speeches, the crowd would be "seeded" with gunman, some obvious and some covert. Trying to apprehend a key leader during a speech would bring too much chaos and collateral damage to the mission. Besides contending with the gunman, the crowd could go either way. They could run or worse, fight and start a riot. The only recourse would be to cut them down. By doing so, you would provide a great deal of political ammunition to the other side because their media was there to record all the events that occurred. As rallies go, there would probably be numerous cameras, photographers and media there to catch the blow-by-blow action that unfolded. Even though it was possible to neutralize the right security people, as soon as they were down, someone else would pick up their weapon and try and engage you. Now, there is a body on the ground, in civilian clothes, riddled with bullets and no weapon in sight. It would provide a great one-sided media story of how U.S. forces "slaughtered" innocent civilians. No, we would have to wait and try and find a better location.

As the day wore on, things started to pick-up in the afternoon. Intel from a "source" (snitch/paid informant) began to come in reference key staff members of the local militia. They were to have a meeting shortly at a local commanders house. The source was to give a prearranged signal next to the commander's location, which would start our deliberate planning cycle. Until he did this, there was not much we could do. As the source started getting closer to the target building, Team Leaders (TL's) were advised, got dressed and headed for the TOC. This sent a non-verbal signal to the Assistant Team Leaders (ATL's) that something was a foot and to upgrade their relaxed state of dress to one of combat.

The signal was given and we planned a hasty assault on this target. The structure was a multiple story building. We did our best to find the front door to the target and adjust our plan and assets accordingly. We sketched out our plan and got the word to move to the birds. As we started our final brief with the pilots and the team, we got the word that the target had changed. We moved back to the TOC and were briefed that the snitch was too scared to give the signal in front of the right building and did it about a block away because of overt security and gunman on the ground. He was told to move next to the right building and give the signal. He did and we began our second planning session. This time, the building was easy to see, but the main entrance was not. We had planned for it being in the front, but once on the ground, we found that it was not.

The command gave the word to go and we moved to the birds, re-briefed and climbed on the pods. We stood by until the entire package was ready and watched as the now routine flight took formation. The lead birds lifted and you could feel the engine rev and the blades start biting air as your platform lurched forward to take its spot in the armada. We flew out over the water and then made a right turn over the countryside and back over the city. As we picked up our heading, I started looking for check points and began to orient myself with the route. I scanned below and ahead for threats and looked further ahead for the target building, keying off the actions of the lead birds. I got the one finger minute signal from our pilot and we unhooked our safety lines knowing that we were inbound. We were planning on landing in pairs, two and two, but the area was too tight for the two birds and the second bird drifted back and took our slot. Our pilot decided that we could not fit and pulled out of the formation and did a quick loop and brought us back around. It only took a about a minute and I found myself looking for targets and threats as we made our way around.

By this time, three birds had deposited their teams and were lifting off. This left us with plenty of room to insert. I remember looking at the target building directly in front of me as we drifted to the ground and seeing that the building had two flat roofs with a parapet and open type patios. I was worried that someone might pop out and fire on us as they had sufficient time to prepare for our presence. We exited the pods and headed for what we thought was the front door. As we closed on our breach point, I had a local male in my way that did not seem too concerned that we were there. I scanned him for weapons and dropped him with a leg strike/sweep. I wanted to get into his personal space and wanted to ensure him and others around that we were not screwing around.

As we closed on the breach point, it was an open door that led into a small warehouse of some sort. There were pallets of food and grain stacked up in several areas around the floor. One of our sister teams was already inside looking for the entrance to the residence that we were supposed to be hitting. It was not in there. I took the team outside and looked to my left, and along the wall were one room deep shops to the corner, about 25 yards away. This is when I first noticed the AK fire was starting to pick up. Someone was shooting at us, but they were air balls, too high to discern the sonic crack of the round. We moved past the shops and rounded the corner. We immediately found an open gate to our left and glancing in, saw the entrance to the target building.

The steps went up about five feet from ground level. I led in and went up the steps and caught site of a man from bird two, pulling rear security for the team as they cleared. I did not hear gunfire, which indicated to me that they were not in contact and asked if the upper floor had been cleared. He said "no" and I told my guys to go upstairs. We moved quickly up the stairs and into the beginning of a short hallway. The point called for a banger and we flash banged the hallway and cleared the first room on the right. The room contained only a mattress. As Scott moved past a window, he caught a burst of SAW (Squad Automatic Weapon) fire from a friendly blocking position about 25 yards east on the corner.

Some of the rounds narrowly missed his head and most impacted on the outside of the window on the side of the building. We then cleared a small patio to our left and then turned right, out onto a flat open roof that was surrounded by a three-foot concrete slotted wall or parapet. As we broke out, I caught sight of a fireball about two blocks to the north from behind a concrete lattice-work on top the roof of a building that was the same height as ours. The fireball was produced by a gunman firing an AK at us as we came out of the roof door. Kim, who was behind me in the stack, later told me the gunman was hitting the doorway above our heads, probably because he was shooting full auto and his muzzle was rising. I broke right with Kim while Tony and Scott broke left and began engaging the gunman. I told the guys to stay down and not to break the visual plane of the parapet wall. I was more worried about friendly fire than I was the bad guys. As I took a knee and rolled my back into the parapet, an M60 machine gun from another position began chewing up the wall on the other side of where Kim and I were hunkered down. Evidently the gunner had seen and heard Tony and Scott's muzzle blast and thought it was bad guys shooting at them. Everyone hit the deck and I could see Norm getting ready to break out on to the roof behind us through the same door we exited. I gave him a hand and arm signal to hold and he could see that we were under fire.

I got on the command net and called the assault commander. I told him to tell the blocking positions to stop firing at us on the target building. Evidently, things were hot on the street and the battle positions were taking fire. The perimeter commander had the bright idea during rehearsals and training to put 1LT's in charge of the battle positions and made the more qualified platoon sergeants almost become a non-player. This may work when no one is shooting at you, but when the game is on, that is what squad and fire team leader are for, to control their elements. One LT. cannot control the visual input and physical output of 15 different soldiers at one time. Only properly trained personnel can accomplish this mission.

We crouched and ran back into the target building and moved downstairs to see if the initial team needed any help. We went to work re-clearing all the rooms and helping them consolidate all the prisoners. We counted 22 people that were on the target, none offering any resistance. As we did our secondary clears, I found a computer and monitor. The computer itself was too big to bring back, especially during a firefight, so I pumped shotgun rounds into the monitor and the box to destroy it. Once we concluded our secondary clear of the bottom floor, the prisoners were consolidated into the courtyard by the team who had apprehended them. The commander said that vehicles were in route to pick us up and our prisoners.

I could not see squat from the courtyard and not wanting to stay in the gaggle that was forming. I took the team up to the roof and helped with the blocking positions with the mounting fire that the teams were facing. We moved back upstairs and went into the first room that we had cleared and taken fire from. It had a window facing South and East and we could maintain a good visual on a hotel across the street. Tony and Scott took the South window while Kim and I took the East. Looking out the South window, about half a block down the street was a corner with a tree in front of it. The blocking position below us then lit up the corner with rifle fire. I saw a man poke his head out and then retreat. I watched the man reappear in the courtyard and he began yelling back and forth to a woman that appeared to be his wife. I could not see a weapon in his hand and he might have left it at the corner where he had been shot at a few moments before. He soon disappeared and I pointed to the corner and told Kim to hit it with a 40mm round. He was unsure of where I was talking about, so I launched four to five tracer rounds at the wall next to the corner.

Kim picked up on my rounds and launched a high explosive round down range. The round hit in the "Y" of the tree, exploding and blowing every leaf off. I thought I could hear the blocking position below us cheer and the man never did poke his head out around the corner again. As I continued my scan to the left, I could see a helicopter hovering and men fast roping to the ground. Suddenly, a cloud of smoke expanded from the tail and I heard the report of the explosion. The bird shook and wavered........

# AFTER ACTION COMMENTS

### Sustain:

- Maintain momentum once the assault has begun and keep clearing until you find the target.
- Be aware of both friendly and enemy fire.
- Do not "gaggle," there is always something you and your team can contribute, even if it is only pulling security.

### Improve:

- Conduct coordination and rehearsals with friendly units and ensure discrimination and rules of engagement are adhered to.

# THE KEY TO CONSISTENT SUCCESS

I have found that the key to consistent success in small and large-scale operations to rest on the shoulders of the Tactical Team Leader. The team's performance, training, motivation, and attitude are a direct reflection of the team leader's drive and professionalism. When properly selected, trained and resourced, they will ensure the mission is accomplished in a swift and efficient manner. Fortunately for me during my team leader time, I inherited a team of warriors, which made my job almost effortless.

Why the team leader? By referring to S.L.A Marshal's accounts of Squad Leadership in WWII in his book, "Men Against Fire," he determined the fire team is the most effective span of control for the combat leader at ground level. To help solve the span of control problem, one must first understand the team size in a tactical environment. In volatile heavy combat and under high stress ("bombs are bursting, the bullets are flying and people are dying"), four to six personnel are the typical maneuver element. This is what combat veterans of WWII, Korea and Vietnam I have spoken to, come to agree on. Why? Again, we must train and prepare for the worse case scenario, that being, the noise and confusion of the battlefield. Marshall pointed out that the span of control decreases with the chaos of battle. The veterans with whom I have spoke with remark that when the bullets start flying, you can only effectively control and maneuver four to six. They said the platoon and squad combat elements routinely broke down into small groups firing and maneuvering on an enemy position.

Much of the problem results from the auditory exclusion that sets in as a result of the shooting. The noise of the battlefield is deafening. I can remember wearing ear plugs when going into combat to help retain my hearing when things calmed down. You see, the firing will eventually cease and the bad guys will try probing you by quietly sneaking in. If you have not protected your hearing, it makes it a bit easier for the enemy to close on you. Because of your hearing loss, you are now only using 50 percent of your senses to scan with. The other 50 percent is your vision. While scanning is effective in locating enemy personnel, many times what keys you into looking in a particular direction is sound. Taking away that very important sense is an unnecessary handicap. Especially with today's sophisticated electronic hearing amplification and protection devices which can now protect your hearing and amplify the important sounds on the battlefield.

Assuming that you have lost your hearing, you now only have your vision to observe, assess and control the battlefield. This also applies to your men and getting their attention. They must be continually scanning to catch your hand and arm signals or you must move to them and scream in an already deafened ear. Another problem is that men are taught to spread out when they are getting shot at, generally three to five meters from each other. With their spreading out, and you protecting yourself from incoming fire, you will be strained to see two people to your right and two to your left at all times. In the forest or jungle, vegetation will hamper your line of sight. In an urban environment, any ninety-degree turn a team member takes will block your vision of him and his status. Again, this is your worse case scenario span of control that we must prepare for.


## TEAM MAKE UP

The make-up of any tactical team needs to be simple, efficient and compliment the tactical element. A sample team structure that follows can apply to military or the law enforcement tactical team:

Team Leader (TL)
Assistant Team Leader (ATL)
Breacher

Medic

Less Lethal

Gumby

All members of the tactical team are trigger pullers first, meaning that they all carry a primary (rifle) and back-up (pistol) weapon in addition to their specialty gear. Some for example, may carry extra equipment. A breacher carries a manual breaching tool such as a ram or halligan as part of their team responsibility, they would still carry both a rifle and a pistol. Some will argue that this is too much equipment and that only a sidearm should be carried in the above case. I disagree. For military operations, I prefer the breacher to be a completely interchangeable part of the team and this will require both weapon systems. Sometimes a small range of missions may also require the officer or soldier to carry a pistol as a primary weapon. Even in this circumstance, I would require them to carry a second pistol as a back up should their primary pistol fail. This mindset dovetails into the layered offense mindset and the principle of always carrying a backup weapon. As for the men who want to carry pistols as primary entry weapons, they will argue that they can cover and do the job with a pistol, but I remain skeptical. A quick trip to the range by the team leader will find this out whether this person is lazy and trying to get over or if they can really do the job with their sidearm alone.

Team leader (TL) duties require practice and experience. A team member should have several years of seasoning in tactical operations before being selected to the team leader position. It would be a good idea for the individual to first spend one to two years as an Assistant Team Leader (ATL) , to validate and polish out any needed skills and learn all the aspects of the job. Assistant team leaders will generally get the needed experience as they are generally in charge of the team during the TL's absence. Besides the temporary leadership roles, the ATL needs to know how to perform all the same duties of the TL to include tactical planning and leadership counseling. Occasionally during training scenarios it is wise to "kill off a TL" and require the ATL take over and accomplish the mission.

At the lower end of the team is the team breacher. The breacher is probably the most important person in the stack. If you can't get in to your target, you can't have mission success. I think it is smart to have the newest member of the team become the team breacher for one to two years.  Why?  Everyone on the team needs to know how to breach should the breacher be hurt or killed during an operation.  Anyone, including the TL, should be able to pick up a breaching tool and breach a door in an emergency situation.  Also, if the team gets split up into a two and three person element, you can have a breaching capable shooter with each group.  Routinely in the law enforcement arena the biggest person on the team becomes the breacher and they are saddled with the job until the next hulk arrives.  This is primarily due to manual breaching being the primary breaching means for forced entry.

Next on the team are the specialty skills that team members need to possess in order to be a diversified asset.  These skills can be medical, less lethal or communications, the latter depending on how sophisticated your communications program is.  As with breacher skills, medical skills are equally as important.  The first responder to a medical situation is generally going to be you.  Whether you are injured, your buddy, a hostage or innocent, you will be the first one to provide medical treatment.  Everyone on the team should carry basic medical supplies and know how to use them.

The common rational is to let the dedicated medic handle the injury.  The reality is that the team medic or dedicated medic may not be able to get to the injured person because of the intensity of fire.  The first priority should go to neutralizing the threat and then caring for the injured, otherwise more friendly forces will be at risk.  One dead or injured body does not justify two.  Once the bad guy(s) are taken care of the easiest way to stop the bleeding is to put direct pressure on the wound or a tourniquet.  Someone else will probably be cutting clothing, exposing the wound and getting bandages out.  Pretty quick you will have two to three people working on one gun shot wound.

For ease and efficiency of treatment, everyone should have the same medical package and training.  The team medic should be the subject matter expert for the team and may carry a few more bandages should the situation require it.  In the law enforcement arena, it is just as critical to be medically trained and proficient because emergency medical service (EMS) personnel generally cannot come into a target until the entire area is secure. In the case of an active shooter scenario, such as the Columbine High School incident, you had scores of innocent victims that needed immediate treatment. I tell my LE classes that killing the bad guys is easy, but when it is accomplished is when the real work begins. Individual officers are generally the first responders to an active shooter situation and once they have security and have neutralized the threat, they should immediately revert to providing medical support. This is where the real life saving work will begin. Rapid hands on to prevent blood loss is the key.

Next, if there are any specialty missions that a team needs such as less lethal, chemical or shields, then the team should have a dedicated expert to turn to. With the variety of equipment available, there is a great deal of information that needs to be tracked and passed to team members to keep them on the cutting edge. Law enforcement teams are saddled with multiple layers of less lethal taking the form of hand held gas, gas launchers, Tasers and much more. Proper employment techniques require proper training and certification. This will also come into play when starting collective training with various teams.

Finally, sniper teams can maintain the same generic structure as the average assault team, but will add their special skills to the mix. I prefer to select snipers who have proven themselves as assaulters for at least two years. This seasoning allows the new sniper to understand the importance of reporting correct and accurate information to the command and assault elements. Having breached multiple barriers as an assaulter, the new sniper will know what information is critical when reporting breach points instead of passing a bunch of fluff or useless information. Snipers will also know that when they perform their area recons, the important information such as routes and obstacles that an assault team will encounter when approaching a target. Sniper teams have the ability to break down into to two sub shooting teams for tactical operations in permissive environments such as your local communities. For the woods, I prefer to keep the sniper elements as a package, four to six personnel, so they can provide their own security and put up a better fight while in Indian country.

## TEAM LEADER SELECTION

The Team Leader (TL) should be selected from proven Assistant Team Leaders (ATL's), those who have consistently and successfully led a team or part of a team in the Team Leader's absence. ATL's should be able to run a team in the absence of a TL and should have the same qualities and attributes of their leader. If a TL is injured, killed, removed for cause or it is just his time to rotate, the senior ATL should be selected to fill the vacancy. Should the group consist of both Sniper and Assault teams, you might want to put an assaulter in an assault position and a sniper in a sniper TL role. Generally, these individuals are specialized by this time and they will be more efficient in their specialty field. Occasionally, you can cross-pollinate the teams if the individual has a willingness to change over. While serving in Special Operations, it became the goal of every operator to stay in an "Action Guy" (AG) status as long as possible before rotating to an instructor job and getting away from the action and door kicking. Once you become an instructor, you would be known as a FAG or Former Action Guy. As I saw my time approaching to become a TL, it meant that after two years of service in that position, I would be sent to an instructor slot. So, I volunteered to do two years as a sniper. This would give me two more years in the trenches and the possibility of participating in a few more real world missions.

Being a sniper gives also gives you the best of both worlds. Having paid their dues as an assaulter for two years, they can do both sniping, tactical reconnaissance or assault work as needed. It was literally the best job I had, next to team leader. As I rose to the Assistant Team Leader position on a sniper team, the team leader of the assault team I grew up on was killed in a parachute accident. I was selected to return to this team as a team leader.

It was a tough and solemn time for awhile. I knew all of the men on the team and they were exceptional individuals. The loss of Bubba, was devastating. They allowed me back into his position and I quietly took control of the team. I simply had to sit the guys down one day and let them know it was all right to grieve and that I understood. I also let them know that I was not Bubba and that I wanted to learn their system of doing business versus changing five people to my way of thinking. It is much easier that way. My job as a TL was to get the job accomplished as smart and safely as possible. If they did not violate any security protocols with their tactics, I had no problem with how they accomplished the mission. You see, in Special Ops, each group may have a slightly different way of doing things like tactics and planning. There is no problem with this and they must be allowed their "creativity" if you will, to figure out the best way to get things done.

A pitfall for team leader selection is appointing team leaders for anything other than their performance. This can be disastrous. I have witnessed this first hand in both the Special Operations and law enforcement community where friendship, gender or ethnic appointments had life endangering results. In Special Ops, we had one individual who had the rank, but did not have the skill or the talent to do the job. The command appointed him to a TL position and he ran the team into the ground, morale wise. Finally, after an issue with a travel voucher, they sent him away from the unit to another special forces group where he proceeded to screw up a special forces "A" Team. Instead of solving the problem, they flushed it to another area of the Army for someone else to solve.

In the law enforcement arena, I am aware of an incident where an unqualified politically appointed team leader pushed a hard hit on a barricaded person, where it was not needed. The bad person was justifiably neutralized, but in the process, a friendly officer was shot and permanently crippled. This is unacceptable. Out of this one incident, the team has already lost five individuals. This could have been easily avoided by properly selecting a team leader from within the ranks. Too many times organizations put restrictions on where team leaders come from and appoint TL's from outside the tactical unit. Once in awhile it will work with the right individual, but generally it is a recipe for disaster. The team generally has to re-train the team leader in tactics and techniques, wasting precious time and reinventing the wheel. Proven experience should have been a prerequisite for their initial appointment. In effect, the team who has to re-train a team leader has to take two-steps backward before they progress.

## TEAM LEADER DUTIES

Simply put, the success or failure of the team lies on the shoulders of the Team Leader. Their success is your success, their failure, your failure. A TL's first job should be to get to know the team and assess their strengths and weaknesses. The getting to know part should be easy with personal counseling sessions.  The assessment part will depend on the training schedule and the variety of upcoming training.  By simply conducting routine range fire, you can begin to evaluate their individual skills.  Simply by doing a team run and physical training session, you will build morale and it will give you an idea of their physical preparedness.

Once you're assigned the role, my suggestion is to come in quiet and watch for a period of time.  Again, I have found it easier to learn the team's standard operating procedures (SOP's) than to try and change everything at once and start from scratch.  If their drills are sound, why not stick with them.  You will have time during your assignment as team leader to slowly change things that you disagree with.  Massive change from the start will only be met with mental resistance.  Team members will either think that your have no faith in them, their tactics or techniques.  If the tactics are unsafe nor sound, by all means change them.  But don't change them to show them who is boss.  This is an ego problem that you should have fixed at the individual level.  Not only is the change silly, but counter productive to the team morale and growth.  Training time is a precious commodity and should not be wasted.

As a new TL, you should come in early and stay late on your own, reviewing the team's SOP's and checking out equipment, etc.  You might quietly inspect the condition of the team's equipment, weapons, vehicles, etc., to get a better feel for their preparedness level.  Ask questions of team members about their team specialty in a non-threatening way, so the team member your talking to feels they are educating you versus being put on the spot.  Also, by coming early and staying late, you get to see who is doing the same.  You will get a better feel for the personnel on your team and their strength's and weaknesses.

## THE ADMINISTRATIVE TEAM LEADER

The administrative side of the team leader can be as equally as important at the combat or the training side.  Up until the last couple of years, the military Special Ops were not killing a terrorist everyday.  Most of their time was spent on routine day-to-day training.  Keeping up with volumes of paperwork the military and law enforcement require can be a constant chore.  You owe it to yourself and team to learn to type and to run basic computer software programs to ensure that you can efficiently handle the required paperwork. Most action guys will call this a sacrilege, but if you learn to become more efficient with training schedules, evaluations, awards and after action reports, the more time you will be able to spend on the range with the team doing the important stuff like training and rehearsals.

You also assume a moral and professional obligation to ensure that your team is taken care of in regards to yearly evaluations and promotions. As a Reserve Officers Training Corps (ROTC) instructor, I saw cadets commissioned that did not write a term paper in their four years of college. I was shocked. The problem that comes with the inability to write is that you cannot properly describe on paper with accurate detail how good or bad your team members are. This is especially important when your team members are competing for promotion against other officers or service members. Generally they are not competing against each other, but rather how well their supervisors can project thoughts and ideas on paper. I have seen numerous individuals in my career suffer because they had a supervisor who could not articulate a clear thought on their subordinates evaluations.

Evaluations suffered as did individual awards. Those afraid of writing were also reluctant to put their people in for awards because of their poor writing habits. When they did put in awards, their narratives were generally too weak, or poorly written to support the recommendations. Awards were kicked back or downgraded and who suffered? The individual. As luck would have it, the unschooled team leader would generally have a great boss that could write and their evaluations would never suffer. The TL would continue their attitude and demeanor of non-education or self-improvement in this area, smugly getting promoted, thinking "I got mine" or that the administrative stuff is not for an "action guy" like me. This piss poor attitude only trickled down and screwed over their subordinates.

## THE TEAM LEADER AS A TRAINER

Training for success in all assigned missions is the primary goal of the team leader. Ensuring team members are on the cutting edge will help ensure their survival and the survival of the team in a high-risk situation. Through your initial assessment of the team, you should have noted any deficiencies in their training or skills and prioritized which training is the most urgent. Generally, training that will save them from death or great bodily injury will be the first priority. Many times something as simple as weapons or training safety will be a good start. Many leaders have found that as a result of a training accident, training of all types will come to a screeching halt. Not as much in the military, but in the law enforcement arena, an accidental shooting can halt effective training for years while all the fingers point and litigation runs it's course.

It is of the utmost importance that the team leader, the ATL and the entire team constantly monitor safety, especially with units dealing with weapons and live fire training. A simple system of checks and balances needs to be established to ensure that no one is hurt or injured. Also as important is setting the example for your team members to follow. The team leader needs to set the example with safety, weapon handling and discrimination. Once you develop your safety routine, you can then properly execute high-risk training. This system should extend and dove-tail into flat range fire, live fire close quarter battle (CQB) and then to combat with little or no changes.

Start by looking at the collective team skills and decide which ones the team needs to work on the most. Use all the assets available to ensure you maximize your training time and effort. What many leaders forget, is that you do not have to be the subject matter expert in all areas, you simply have to manage them. For example, for internal team training, you can task out members of the team to set-up, rehearse and execute training for your element. If medical training is your priority, task the team medic to set-up and deliver the training. Using this technique will spread out the responsibility and require each person to know the subject matter they are going to teach. If they fail to put out a good block of instruction, it will readily show in the training and generally the peer pressure will ensure that they are not unprepared again. The TL also can verbally or in writing counsel the person responsible for the training.

A simple technique to begin this process is for the team leader to plan, prepare and execute the first block of training to set the standard for future team training. This will take away all the excuses from team members in future training when you get the occasional comment stating that they did not know what was expected. The TL should ensure that all classes, presentations, demonstrations and handouts are to standard and he should use this as a teaching point to ensure the team understands what is expected of them in the future. And, in the future, the TL should be briefed by the individual tasked to perform the training, to ensure it adequately covers the desired information. This will help maximize each and every training day.

As a final point in team leadership, the Team Leader should require team members to step forward at all times on their own and take initiative. Whether it be something as simple that needs to be done like cleaning up team equipment or someone rising to a tactical leadership challenge, operation personnel should understand that setting the example is the right thing to do. Members should not be penalized for stepping forward and taking initiative. They should be rewarded for it. Too many times members are scolded or chastised for taking initiative. This will stifle initiative and aggressiveness and will result in a wait-and-see attitude in combat, which can be extremely counter productive.

## THE TACTICAL TEAM LEADER

The transition from training leadership to tactical combat leadership should be transparent. "Live the example" in training and mirror what you're going to do in combat. Adhering to this philosophy will make your transition to the battlefield seamless. If you have built a realistic training system that mirrors combat and you train to exceed the standards, you will do well. The only change is that you may lose people. I understand this can happen in training when individuals are injured from time to time, but combat will induce more permanent losses.

As a team leader, understand the concept of "Risk vs. Gamble." Look at your training, your battle drills and combat, with the understanding that there will always be some risk involved. Never gamble or just throw the dice and wish for a happy outcome. Choose tactics that are simple and safe to execute and will ensure the greatest chance of survival for your men. We do a dangerous job and the team needs to understand this. This is why we carry guns, wear layered bulletproof material and all the protective equipment we do. People will shoot at us and will try and do us harm. As a team leader, be smart about when you have to push the fight and when you should not push. We can be at the top of our game and still get killed from an un-zeroed AK in the hands of a child two blocks away. When it is time to get after it, do so with all your heart and assets. Sometimes though, step back and ask if this is the smartest course of action. Don't be afraid to get independent opinions from your men or other team leaders.

As a final point, the Team Leader is the first line of fighting leadership. You need to be technically and tactically proficient with all your weapon systems and set the standard for the newbie on the team. They should aspire to be like you one day. If you "live the example," you set the stage for success. You also take away all the excuses, should anyone want to fall back on one.

## TEAM LEADER TIPS

Rotate team leader planning responsibilities once you have become proficient and skilled at planning team and group assaults on targets. Begin by bringing your ATL with you to planning sessions and allowing them to see the process and expose them to what is going on. Say, every third or forth planning session, start with your ATL and assign them the job of target planning for your team under your supervision. Once your ATL understands the basic planning concepts and requirements, start grooming another team member by exposing them to the process which allows them to see how the process works. Some team leaders see this knowledge as power and wish to keep their lower team members in the dark and ignorant of what goes on. Exposing them to the system is the best way to help develop subordinates into future leaders. In the near future, you may be losing an ATL who has been selected to take over a team. If you have a replacement in mind, start bringing them into the leadership planning cycle early and get them involved in the mission planning process.

As with the exposure to leadership planning, rotate team duties and responsibilities every two to three years to round out everyone on the team and to prevent burn out. As suggested before, rotate everyone first through the position of breacher and then give them a change of pace with either medical or less lethal. This will help prevent burn out and give the individuals a chance to refocus and excel in another area. Also, as a breacher, you routinely enter the room last and never get a shot at the number one or two-man position on entry. Another positive point about bringing the new team member as the breacher, is the TL has the chance to evaluate and assess the new officer for one to two years. Some organizations have a one-year probation time for new personnel and this allows the TL to do a proper assessment. It also gives the new team member a job that is important, but not the immense pressure of running point. Running point requires a seasoned individual who is consistent and has been exposed to all the possible situations that one can run into. In effect, the point person is running the team for a short time in lieu of the team leader.

For control purposes, find the best place to control your team. Some feel it is up front, but I suggest a place in the middle of the stack so as to see both the front and rear of the team. The team leader should ensure all members of the team are trained to the highest level because on fast moving tactical operations, contact can be made anywhere and by any member of the stack. For this reason, everyone from the point person to the rear guard needs to be dialed in and ready to do business.

Further, as a team leader, I use a system where my team members put hands on and either I cover or supervise. This is important because if I get caught putting hands on, I am not doing my job as a leader. My job is to supervise my team and ensure that we maintain 360 degree security at all times. Wrapping someone up with flex ties and searching them does not allow me to do this. Some times you will find yourself in this position, but team members should be trained to see this, step in and take over, freeing me up to do my job.

## TEAM LEADERSHIP

- Live The Example For Your Team To See.
- Avoid Putting Hands On As A Team Leader.
- Understand And Apply "Risk Vs. Gamble."
- Continually Train Your Junior Leaders To Fill The Next Position.

# CHAPTER SIX

# ORGANIZATIONAL LEADERSHIP

*"We trained hard…but it seemed that every time we were beginning to form up into teams we would be reorganized. I was to learn later in life that we tend to meet any new situation by-reorganizing; and what a wonderful method it can be for creating the illusion of progress while producing confusion, inefficiency and demoralization."*

Peter Arbiter, Roman Legionnaire, 210 B. C.

- DEFINITION OF AN ORGANIZATIONAL LEADER
- SELECTION OF THE ORGANIZATIONAL LEADER
- ROLE OF THE ORGANIZATIONAL LEADER
- TECHNIQUES OF LEADERSHIP
- PROBLEMS OF ORGANIZATIONAL LEADERSHIP
- WHEN TO SAY NO
- TEST AND EVALUATION OF NEW EQUIPMENT
- ENSURE THE COMMUNICATION PROCESS IS WORKING BOTH WAYS

## BAD DOGS

Our next new target came to us via some disgruntled neighbors. While sitting on one target, waiting for another intel hit to come our way, some locals from the neighborhood came to our position and informed us that the people who lived next door to their residence were part of the bad guys militia. We assembled our group, made a hasty plan and headed out on foot to our new target. We moved two or three blocks, made a left hand turn and the target was the second house on the left. Our team's mission was to move to the back of the residence and secure it. As was normal for the area, the house's yard was surrounded by a five-foot concrete wall. We did a hasty clear of the back yard visually over the wall. . Being the number one man, I was then boosted over the wall. The "T" post from a clothes line was an arms reach further than I could manage and I dropped onto a wooden chair that someone had placed against the inside of the wall. Upon contacting the chair, my feet went through it and now I had the ring of the seat around my legs. "Not a good start," I thought. I stepped out of the chair and took up a security position while the rest of the team maneuvered over the wall. Once in the yard, the fun began. Teams started hitting the front side of the house and it awoke three dogs in the backyard with us. The dogs decided they were going to do their job and protect the yard and headed toward us, the new strangers in their world. As one got close to Gary, he fired off a 5.56 round close to the lead dog's head. The muzzle blast from the Car-15 is wicked and all three decided they did not want to play with the strangers. They ran up the back steps to the house and huddled together shivering, still wondering what the boom was all about. We penetrated through the back door of the residence and linked up with the team on the inside. Coming back out, we ran into another team who was placing a charge on a locked door directly around the corner from the stairs and the dogs. The blast channel and overpressure was about to come around and give the dogs another dose of sensory overload. The team called burning and we all took cover, everyone except for the dogs. The charge went off and the blast wave hit them and that was all she wrote. They were last seeing hauling ass south past a blocking position. The target turned out to be a dry hole. No guns, equipment, uniforms or anything to indicate that bad guys lived there. As best we could figure, our informants were the neighbors that had a beef with the those who lived in the house we just finished remodeling. We aim to please. Not a door was left intact and the vehicles had a few more holes than when we started.

During this series of operations, simple and common sense decisions by our commander, allowed us to shed our heavy vests. We were able then to conduct numerous missions such as the one just described. We developed simple SOP's, such as keeping a one-quart canteen on your belt or in the cargo pocket of your pants and drinking it prior to a hit. Once the target was secure, you would refill and drink several more while pulling security and waiting for intel to designate a new target. This enabled us to conduct raids on demand without going in burned out or too tired to properly focus.

## AFTER ACTION COMMENTS

### Sustain:

- Don't be afraid to make smart decisions using the "Risk vs. Gamble" philosophy.

### Improve:

- Be careful of old wooden chairs

## DEFINITION OF AN ORGANIZATIONAL LEADER

The term "Organizational Leader" is a generic term that I will use to describe a leader who is not in the first line of fighting leadership such as the team leader, but rather an administrative or tactical commander who supports the force near or afar. Why make this distinction? Because the men at the tip of the spear see this distinction and see a difference. Typically, they see these leaders in a different light. These leaders have different jobs to accomplish in peacetime and combat. Organizational leaders also follow a different selection, training and career path. Both the job of the team leader and an organizational leader are equally important and deal with supporting the troops. They should work closely together to accomplish the mission. Who controls the planning, support and equipment? It should be a combination of the tactical team leader and the organizational leader. The organizational leader's role is not to dictate policy to those going through the door, but rather to help facilitate their actions.

## SELECTION OF THE ORGANIZATIONAL LEADER

Selection of the organizational leader should be similar to that of a team leader. If you have a good system that works, apply it equally across the board. My first choice would be to promote from within and directly from the team leader ranks. Many will argue that it needs to be an officer that has gone through all the proper leadership gates to get there. I disagree. Leadership is leadership and there should be one standard for both enlisted and officers. There has always been a visible division and rift between the NCO's and the Officer ranks and I doubt if it will ever change, until will change the selection and training system for officers. If you asked any performer in the field, who they would rather have lead them in a high-risk environment, the person with four years of college or the person with four years of experience, the answer is simple.

I do not see the entrenched system of leadership in the military changing in the near future, so we will probably have to work with what we have. If the organizational leader is to lead or command troops, then their selection criteria should be based on just that, experience and leadership in that chosen field. Military Special Operations has done a better job at selecting and integrating officer leadership than some of their counterparts in the regular Army and in the law enforcement community. Generally, Special Operations forces require their leadership to endure the same selection process as the enlisted men. Once this is complete, they then branch out to their separate tracks in their chosen profession. An advantage the military has over law enforcement is the way soldiers are immersed in leadership from day one of their enlistment. Fire team and squad leaders are selected as well as platoon sergeants and platoon leaders in basic training. Leadership principles are pushed down to lower levels throughout the initial training process.

# ROLE OF THE ORGANIZATIONAL LEADER

Simply put, the role of the organizational leader is to best support the men in the arena. It is not to micro-manage or over control these men, as this will only slow down your ability to move through Boyd's loop during training and tactical operations. Responsibility, trust and empowerment need to be pushed down to the fighters and team leaders at all times to ensure mission success with the least amount of casualties. Span of control is important at the team level, but it is now mental control that needs to be discussed. Combat consists of team leaders solving individual problems at their level to accomplish a desired collective goal. The most efficient way to do this is to let the individual teams concentrate and focus on solving one problem at a time where time is critical. If an organizational leader attempts to "over control" a battle or exercise, they will not be able to process all the information coming in and time will be lost. Delegating responsibility and authority down to the team level will ensure that the teams move through Boyd's loop quicker and with more efficiency.

# TECHNIQUES OF LEADERSHIP

As with a new team leader, the organizational leader should come in soft and quiet unless it is obvious that the organization is in critical need of repair and that combat operations are imminent. Even then you should maintain the perception of being quiet, professional, observant and forceful to set the stage for positive future leadership. As with the loud talkers and braggers that we previously discussed, leaders will be marked the first time they let their "alligator mouths overload their hummingbird asses." Troops will loose faith and confidence and it will be difficult to maintain a positive role.

# PROBLEMS OF ORGANIZATIONAL LEADERSHIP

The two things that I have found lacking with the organizational leader is finding a leader who has the guts to make the hard decisions in peacetime and just call a spade a spade. We are saturated with spineless leaders who do not demonstrate leadership. They are promoted and rewarded for writing about it and not living it. Generally, they do not have the guts to counsel or fire someone who is not living up to standard. A leader must be able to look a subordinate or superior square in the eye and tell them what the problem is and what needs to be fixed. I have watched too many leaders in both Special Ops and the regular Army fail in this respect. Some of the individuals in question were downright cowards, pushed out of jobs without a black mark on their record only to be promoted to a higher level above their peers, because their supervisor did not have the balls to put it down on paper. If a leader cannot look a subordinate in the eye and tell him or her where they are screwing up, they are doing them a disservice.

The quote at the beginning of this chapter deals with another problem that combat soldiers face and if you have spent any time in the military or law enforcement, you have seen it time and time again. Too many changes too close to the game indicates poor planning, preparation, supervision and leadership on the part of the organizational leader. Failing to plan, review your plan and to take input can result in the success or failure of any operation. If a leader changes the plan prior to contact, they either don't have faith in the plan or their men.

Another problem I have frequently seen swept under the carpet is the inability to make decisions. If a leader cannot make a decision in peacetime, he will have a problem when the stress of combat is looking him straight in the eye. I have witnessed this in regards to violence of action required on the battlefield. Leaders who hesitate or don't use all their firepower and assets in training, will hesitate to use them in combat.

Another problem that comes to the surface time to time is that of the one hit wonders. The policy and philosophy that you did it right once and that you have punched the proverbial ticket and then you don't have to consistently perform again applies to this group. As I have stated before, selection is a never-ending process and this rule should apply equally to both the guys on the ground and to the leaders controlling them. If an individual at the team level screws up, they can get their buddy killed or worse, their team. If a leader screws up, they can get multiple teams killed. Why in the hell would we keep promoting a leader that continues to stumble, especially in the tactical arena. Sadly, this is often the case.

I have also found that a strong base can allow a weak leader to survive. A weak or incompetent leader can come in and run a great organization into the ground for two years and then leave to work another position. Typically, the organization, by their professionalism and work ethic, can inadvertently allow this leader to succeed and then be placed into a position of greater influence where they can screw over more people. This is why leaders should look down and take a keen interest in their subordinates and not look to hitch their wagon to the next star.

By the same token, leadership in the military is generally a dual role. I will use the company level for my example. The company leadership consists of a Captain and a First Sergeant that should work closely together. Success for the company can simply be ensured by having one strong leader in either position. You can have a strong Captain and a weak First Sergeant and the company will survive. You can have a strong First Sergeant and a weak commander and the company will still pull through. If you have a weak commander and First Sergeant, the company is doomed. This is probably not too much of a problem in peacetime with the routine admin and exercises, but combat is another story. I watched one company with two weak leaders crumble during combat conditions. It made me sick. The leaders were then sent off without a blemish on their records to get promoted to higher levels of incompetence.

This amounts to a form of protectionism. I have witnessed protectionism of individuals at every level of leadership to include the team level. I remember a Sergeant Major who kept one of his buddies along through out his military career and into his civilian one. The individual in question was a good man, but had the leadership skill and personality of a rock. This guy could piss off a nun with little effort and brought a black cloud to the morale of whatever element he took charge. First it was a team, then it was a platoon sized element, then as a civilian he would piss everyone off in a 360 degree bursting radius. It amazed me that this exceptional Sergeant Major did this, but in the end, the Sergeant Major did not have to work for him.

The same runs true with the officer corps. West Pointers are a group that have a click within a click. No matter how stupid the individual is, it seems to me the Army sees fit to shuffle them around the service and not out. This goes back to my basic rule about being able to make a hard decision in peacetime. If you can't make a hard decision, you're part of the problem. You should probably do a quick check between you legs to see if your manhood or womanhood is still intact. If it is not, you're probably too big a wimp for the job and should get the hell out.

Religion is another problem that I have encountered over the years that has conflicted with successful leadership. I have had commanders that brought religion into areas of command where it was best kept out. We had a commander that overtly promoted religion and had "prayer" breakfasts in the service, generally one hour before the normal meal. One positive thing it did was to get the chow hall open an hour earlier that morning for us heathens. Drifting in the mess hall early, you got a chance to see the "in" crowd. A few that attended this service were the bootlick, cheese eaters that were intent on sucking up to the commander and being part of the "in crowd." You also had some that were honestly trying to find some spirituality and apply it to their lives. Then you had some that were over the edge religious zealots who attempted to push their beliefs on you and anyone in their bursting radius.

I will be short and brief on my views of God. I believe you were put on this earth to do the best you can with what he gave you. To take care of your family and your fellow man as best you can. I believe one should not use God as a crutch as many do, or as a political tool or discrimination factor in military job appointments. Spirituality in a person is best manifested in actions rather than spoken words. I had the opportunity to see an overly religious leader crumble in combat, caught up in his religious beliefs, almost a Boyd's spiritual loop. My guidance to men going into harm's way is simple. Pray before the fight or after the fight, but during the fight, you fight.

Another leadership problem that I have watched manifest itself is the "general factory." As Special Operations grew, so did the leadership slots at the top. Officers became more interested in looking toward the stars, the ones to be placed on their shoulders rather than down at the men who would help earn those stars for them. It was almost heart breaking to see incredible leaders who had been fire-breathing performers in the past, squelched and beaten into submission by the need to conform for promotion. Many feel the need to make general as a measure of success. I won't go as far as saying that they sold their souls, but it was damn close. I feel some of them gave up some of their principles or "bricks" to get the star. My only hope was that they were able to find a glimmer of self-respect and attempt to do good with their new position of power and influence and not continue to backslide and compromise their integrity.

How long should we let organizational leaders stay at the tactical level? I believe three to four years is a good start to ensure the tactical leader is well seasoned and fully understands the capabilities and has seen most of the tactical scenarios play out. Proper leadership takes energy and if the organization is properly managed, three to four years should be the right time to rotate the leader and ensure they get a physical and mental break. Remaining any longer can result in burn-out and regression.

## WHEN TO SAY NO

I believe that leaders who lack the ability to project honesty and candor at all levels, will in time, jeopardize the health and welfare of their men. With all their education and continuing education, leaders need to look at the mission and beyond. They need to look at the "totality" and results of the mission. Somalia is a prime example of a country and mission that we should have said no to. Somalia was a back water nation where the United States had no strategic, economic or political interests. Had the TF Ranger missions been successful, would the outcome been any different? I think not. I personally believe that some in the world need to evolve on their own and that we cannot fight their internal civil wars for them. Military leaders need to be smart enough to realize this.

A simple rule that political and military leaders should apply when sending troops to these conflicts are, "is the cause worthy enough to send their own son or daughter there to fight and die?" If it is not, then you should weigh the cost of sending American forces. If the booger eaters in that region are at a social point of development where all they know is killing, nothing will change with your presence. I have found that they will stop fighting each other and start fighting you. Eventually, you will have to kill most of the problem individuals off to effect any change. Is it worth it? Will the American people support it? I don't know. An indicator to me is that of the target country's people. If the people of the country we are focusing on will not fight for themselves because they do not have the guts, internal drive and belief in their cause, why should we do it for them?

What I am saying in so many words is that our military leaders should not blindly follow orders, but they should look at the mission and beyond and ensure they voice their concerns loudly to our political leaders. If the political leaders fail to listen, the military leader should be prepared to use overwhelming force to protect their troops once they are put into harm's way. More times than not, commanders are weighing the political atmosphere versus the hostile atmosphere when deciding how much force or support to give their soldiers going into the arena.

## TEST AND EVALUATION AND INTEGRATION OF NEW EQUIPMENT

With the flood of new equipment and the ability to procure this equipment, leaders are now forced to pick and choose "off the shelf" items that will ensure combat success and survival on the battlefield. Want versus need must always be weighed and solid tactics must not be replaced by gadgets. If it helps you do your job, fine. If it is to make you look cool, dump it. As we used to joke, how high is the CDI (Chicks Dig It) factor.

During my time in Special Operations, many believed that we had an endless well or whenever the spigot was turned on, new gear would appear. Nothing could be further from the truth. I wore the same heavy Kevlar vest for ten years. 50 percent of my tactical gear was modified to fit the mission. A key item that we requested for years and it finally received them just prior to combat operations, were night vision goggles. We had asked for these after our last major national conflict and commanders looked in other places to spend the money. Finally, shortly prior to deploying on a real world tactical operation, we were issued new goggles. The problem was that we were unable to train with them prior to deployment and we were unsure of how they would hold up in combat. So, we found ourselves modifying helmets and fabricating brackets for our helmets deployed in a foreign threat country. This is not the smartest way to do business. All the while the Army was spouting the phrase "we own the night." Maybe we just rented it for a while. Well, we finally got the systems up and running and they worked well. Because we had a finite amount of these goggles and not any to spare, we elected to not take them on daytime missions because we were afraid of crushing or damaging them on a hit. Eventually, we modified pouches for them with pieces of ethafoam for padding. In later years we were provide with nice molded plastic carriers that kept them intact during the roughest of training and combat missions.

## ENSURE THE COMMUNICATION PROCESS IS WORKING BOTH WAYS

Effective leaders do their best to ensure that a clear, quick and efficient communication process is always available. The chain of command is the routine system used to deliver information to the masses. This ensures that each member in the chain is kept informed of changes and information while it is being passed to the lowest member of the organization. Some information is so important that it must be passed in mass to ensure its timeliness and accuracy. Some leaders choose to put the information out in mass to ensure it is accurate and that it is interpreted in the correct manner with few changes or personal spins on it as it passes down the chain.

This should also apply from the bottom going to the top. I have witnessed some great tactical solutions which came from the bottom rung of the ladder. My job as a leader is to promote and exploit all the brain power of my subordinates. No matter where the idea comes from, if it works, use it.

## KEY POINTS

- KEEP YOUR LEADERSHIP SELECTION GENDER, RACE, AND RELIGIOUS NEUTRAL.
- LEARN TO PROPERLY AND HONESTLY COUNSEL SUBORDINATES AND TO TAKE DECISIVE AND POSITIVE ACTION SHOULD THEIR ACTIONS OR INACTION DICTATE IT.
- KEEP AN OPEN MIND AS TO SUGGESTIONS AND IDEAS, NO MATTER FROM WHAT LEVEL THEY COME.
- KEEP THE LINES OF COMMUNICATION OPEN AND ENSURE CANDOR IS ALLOWED TO SURVIVE.

# CHAPTER SEVEN

# COMBAT LEADERSHIP

## General Black Jack Pershing was born September 13th, 1860 near

Laclede, MS, he died July 15th, 1948 in Washington, D.C. Highlights of his life include:

1891 Prof. of Military Science and Tactics Univer. of Nebraska

1898 Serves in the Spanish-American War

1901 Awarded rank of Captain

1906 Promoted to rank of Brigadier General

1909 Military Governor of Moro Province, Philippines

1916 Made Major General

1919 Promoted to General of the Armies

1921 Appointed Chief of Staff

1924 Retires from active duty Education West Point.

Just before World War I, there were a number of terrorist attacks on the United States forces in the Philippines by Muslim extremists. So General Pershing captured 50 terrorists and had them tied to posts for execution. He then had his men bring in two pigs and slaughter them in front of the now horrified terrorists. Muslims detest pork because they believe pigs are filthy animals. Some of them simply refuse to eat it, while others won't even touch pigs at all, nor any of their by-products. To them, eating or touching a pig, its meat, its blood, etc., is to be instantly barred from paradise (and those virgins) and doomed to hell. The soldiers then soaked their bullets in the pigs blood, and proceeded to execute 49 of the terrorists by firing squad. The soldiers then dug a big hole, dumped in the terrorist's bodies and covered them in pig blood, entrails, etc. They let the 50th man go. And for the next forty-two years, there was not a single Muslim extremist attack anywhere in the world. Maybe it is time for this segment of history to repeat itself, maybe in Iraq? The question is, where do we find another Black Jack Pershing?

- COMBAT LEADERSHIP PERCEPTIONS AND REALITIES
- SELECTING COMBAT LEADERS
- KEEP IT SIMPLE
- MINDSET-COMMIT TO THE SLAUGHTER
- TRAINING VS. COMBAT LEADERSHIP
- BOYD'S LOOP AND EFFICIENT COMBAT LEADERSHIP

## TAKE DOWN

We received an intel hit that the number two man in the organization was spotted being driven in a lone green Fiat sedan. We quickly notified and briefed the force and launched the package. Our package had practiced countless hours on takedowns of this type and we were ready to interdict this or any other vehicle configuration.

As per the plan, the lead bird with snipers spotted the vehicle and engaged it. After a magazine and a half of semi-automatic fire into the engine compartment, the vehicle finally stalled on a side street. The occupants of the vehicle fled in a panic to a nearby house. The homes in this area were upscale, with heavy metal gates and thick masonry walls surrounding their courtyards.

The birds deposited us about one block away and we were looking for the target vehicle. After the initial dust cloud from infil drifted off and the birds departed, we began our movement down the street. Approaching the target intersection, I saw a man laying on the ground next to the wall. The lead teams had bypassed him. He looked to me like a beggar, wearing somewhat raggedy clothes, possibly a cripple that you would see time to time on the street corner. We looked left and saw the empty Fiat sideways in the middle of the street, bullet holes in the hood. We ducked into the first courtyard on the left and observed teams clearing the residence. Having enough teams to clear the target, I told my guys to drag raggedy man in the courtyard for safety and to flex-tie his hands behind his back and then tie one of his feet to his hands so he would not run away or interfere with our assaults. They promptly did this and when they grabbed his left foot to tie it to his hands, his whole leg flopped and his foot damn near hit him in the back of his head. My limited knowledge of the human anatomy and the little voice in my head said that was probably not good. I called for a medic to check the man out. It turned out that raggedy man was the driver for the bad guy we were trying to capture. Evidently, he took a round in the upper femur, severing the bone. He did not make a sound during this entire episode.

We had lost eyes on where the vehicle occupants had gone, so we decided to start clearing each building in the surrounding area. We promptly turned raggedy man over to one of the dedicated medics and headed for a courtyard and house that was just past the green Fiat. We pushed in through the heavy metal gate and I told Tony to take the guys and clear the two-story residence. I pulled security at the inside of the front gate and wanted to keep tabs on where all the teams were to include the support elements. I also wanted to ensure no one back doored us on this target. It appeared that everyone had bomb burst in all directions away from the green Fiat in an effort to pin our target down and not let him get out of the area. From my position I could see the command element being deposited on the roof of the first residence where raggedy man was being treated in the courtyard.

The commanding general, watching this action unfold in the rear, reportedly commented, "how do they know where to go?" It is actually easier than it looks. The bad guys are on foot and they can only move so far so fast. It is a matter of eliminating all possible hiding places as quickly as possible. The ability to take the initiative at team level is what enabled our success on this operation.

AK-47 fire was starting to pick up and an RPG impacted on the outside wall or building next to where I was covering. It rocked the immediate area and rang my bell. Looking down the street away from the Fiat, I could see a woman standing on the left side of the road in an orange flowery dress about a block and a half away. It looked like she had a gun man shooting from between here legs as I could see the dust kicking up from the muzzle as he shot. I thought about tagging her, but I did not know where our support forces were and I figured if she was a threat, they would take care of her. Little did I know, our blocking force was still circling overhead and had not been inserted on this hit. Why, I hadn't a clue. I learned long ago in training, if you're not sure of your target or where friendly forces are, don't shoot.

Tony brought the team back to me and he was carrying a captured AK. The building had been empty of personnel. We quickly stripped the weapon and threw parts in all directions. Scanning the street, I could see that the command group was pointing to a building across the street from me. I could see Ben occasionally pop up and shoot at something in the distance and then point to what appeared to be the building across the street. I was trying to figure out what they were pointing at and was hoping they would throw smoke on the target as we had asked them to do in the past. No such luck. With sporadic AK rounds still flying to include the occasional RPG, we darted across the street in pairs without laying down cover fire. We thought our security forces were out and did not want to accidentally shoot into one of their blocking positions. So, we held our fire and sucked it up and made successful runs in buddy teams.

As I got to the double courtyard gate, it was hastily tied shut with a piece of rag and it made me think we were getting close to our target. Another team had joined us on our left and as we pushed through, they headed for the front door. Seeing this, we headed for the back to ensure no one squirted out of the target. The building was a nice two-story structure and as we rounded the back corner, Kim advised that we had company. They were looking out the back door or what appeared to be a hole in the wall of the residence. I told him to bang it and we threw a diversionary device in. It went off in a second and a half and then we entered. There were eight people in a small room and the banger had done its job. The concrete walls and roof of the structure only amplified the concussion of the flash bang and everyone appeared to be dazed. The team started putting everyone down and I pulled rear security at the door for a minute because I would just be in the way with all the bodies and the clutter. While the guys were going hands on, it was my job as Team Leader to ensure that we had overall security and that the team was focused on the task at hand.

Our sister team pushed through the front of the target and linked up with us. Other teams had converged on the target and were pouring in and heading up stairs. We quickly secured the building and began to consolidate everyone in the front room for identification. The front room was a larger room with better light and we used it as a common meeting place to link-up after the target was secure. As we started to consolidate our prisoners in the first room, a team member of the consolidation team started questioning one of the guests we deposited in the link up point. The person in question blurted out his name to the operator. Bingo, we had him.

We notified the command element that we had our man and requested an exfil. We were advised to use our roof as an exfil point and began to shuttle birds in to retrieve our teams and prisoners. We were still taking fire and in the lulls and we were looking hard through concrete lattice works in the stairwell for someone to shoot at. We could hear the gun birds working some folks over with rockets and mini-guns and knew things were heating up. As the birds came in for us, we postured with our team and quickly mounted the bird with our prisoner to cut down the exposure time.

We lifted off and did our best to look for targets to suppress. We could not see any, but could hear the AK's hammering away at us and our positions. The bad guys were tucked in tight wherever they were. I heard that some were even in trees, but I could not spot any muzzle flashes. It sucked because you wanted to shoot, but you knew you had to maintain fire discipline. To my knowledge, no one on our bird fired because they could not identify any targets and because we did not know where the blocking positions were. Once out of the target area, things quieted down and our pilot deposited us at the front gate of our compound. We secured our prisoner and handed him over to a prisoner of war team who would search him, photograph and prepare to interrogate him.

I got my team together and began our personnel and weapons check. This is routine after an action to ensure no one is hurt or shot and does not know it. With all the adrenaline, guys have taken hits before and did not know it until after the fight. Besides checking to ensure you had all your equipment, you would check yourself and buddy out. After this quick check I would get the teams story straight.  This is not what it sounds like.  When Tony took his residence down, I had no idea what they had done, found or if they had killed any gunman.  This was my time to find out what happened out of my view so I could give an accurate report to the commander.  I did not want something to have happened and not been aware of it, good or bad.

As we entered the debriefing area we were pumped up and happy to be alive.  A couple of guys high-fived, because they were happy to see their buddies were safe and uninjured.  Between snipers and gun birds, they had engaged over 20 bad guys during the hit and this had been the most fire taken to date.

Our commander verbally chastised us, stating, "You men need to settle down, there are some families out there without their loved ones."  He was referring to the bad guys who were trying to kill us.  Emotionless, we looked at each other and you could see the truth in every ones eyes.  The feeling that our commander was near his psychological and emotional edge and that his religious beliefs were getting in the way of his combat decisions.  We had feared this would come to pass because of his past history.  Our commander was a good man, but missed his calling as a Chaplin.  What was worse, was that it appeared that his deep religious beliefs were interfering with his combat decision making abilities.  This would play out later on a large scale later during more critical operations.........

## AFTER ACTION COMMENTS

### Sustain:

- Team leader aggressiveness and initiative.
- Discrimination and weapon employment.

### Improve:

- Better communication as to who is on the ground (support)?

# COMBAT LEADERSHIP PERCEPTIONS AND REALITIES

Many leaders, both non-commissioned officers and officers go into the leadership role with many preconceived notions of what a leader is and how they are supposed to act. We have all seen the typical movie roles of the leader out front, leading the bayonet charge into the enemy. It is a technique, one that I don't really recommend. Effective combat leadership should empower the fighting troops to take initiative and decisive action at the lowest level to support the common goal. Leaders that have properly trained troops and that are self confident in their tactics and capabilities are not afraid to do this. Not all troops are to this level, but this is where we should strive to be.

One must understand that in today's battlefield, we are routinely fighting a "G" or Guerrilla who is lightly dressed in what we would term pajamas, has only an AK-47 and two magazines for it and can run circles around us in our heavy combat gear. We must focus on getting to the better position first before he does, or he will have the advantage. The shooters at ground level must have the latitude to close on and engage these guys on our terms and not theirs. Should we see a weakness, we need to efficiently push through them to superior positions and then call back to our next level of leadership and brief them of our progress. If not, the G will get into the better position first and we will have to try and root him out of his defensive position, which puts you at the disadvantage. Also, one must understand the "window of opportunity" to engage a target in a fast moving gunfight opens and closes very rapidly. You are either mentally, tactically and physically ready to take the shot or you are not. This applies to the lowest level of the team.

# SELECTING COMBAT LEADERS

Selecting leaders who have taken the hard path and gone into harm's way, earning their right to lead is the key to successful leadership. Ticket punchers who think they can easily do the action guy stuff without the prior validation or training is putting their soldiers lives in jeopardy. Special Operations in the Army has seen much of this type of behavior. The actual cutting edge forces are not that vast in number and it seems that everyone and their brother wants to play without going through selection or paying their dues. So, they circumvent the system. They create vast and unwieldy commands and control groups so they can be part of the Special Operations club and put their two cents worth into the equation. Soon, you have ticket punchers in higher headquarters who have never done any time in the arena dictating policy to the shooters. They circumvent the system and worm their way into support and operations sections. Some of these sections don't have savvy leadership and then allow these individuals to hamper or influence the men in the arena. In simple terms, they are a pain in the ass and what we termed "strap-hangers," guys who want to come along and see what the action guys are doing so they can boast to their peers and others that they did this or that.

## KEEP IT SIMPLE

Don't overcomplicate the command and control or checks and balances you use on the battlefield. Simplicity is the key. Remember to rotate your sub unit personnel and missions to give everyone a chance at planning and mission leads. This will keep everyone sharp and focused. Also, keep the lines of communication open and have backup plans, should the primary means fail.

It is critically important that your soldiers know the capabilities of their weapon systems, their safe use and discrimination. With the upgraded lethality of our weapons systems, we cannot afford to have a bad day. I can remember being on several operations and taking fire from unknown personnel. On several of those instances, I could not identify who was shooting at me. By engaging the threat, I would put other friendly troops in jeopardy, so I did not fire. Sometimes you need to find hard cover and look hard during fast moving gun fights to ensure you're putting rounds on the right people. This goes for Special Operations forces as well as conventional forces in today's chaotic foot and mechanized engagements.

# MINDSET-COMMIT TO THE SLAUGHTER

As discussed in the combat mindset chapter, the leader must be as equally stable as the soldiers they are sending into combat and have the same aggressive mindset, but on a larger scale. They need to be mentally ready to commit slaughter on several different targets or in several different areas at the same time. The individual or team leader is going to neutralize threats as they come, usually one at a time. The leadership, on the other hand, is going to be watching this from a command position, bird or even on a television screen.

The leaders mind needs to be right and focused. You may be tasked to target "suspected" enemy positions or civilian positions that the enemy has taken to engage your men. Whether or not civilians are there, those positions need to go away. This seems a simple matter to me, but leaders too far from the fight will put too much thought into this simple scenario. It gets even more complicated when we have to preemptively take out targets that we know are bad. We will have civilian casualties. Such is the case where the bad guys put an air defense site on top of a civilian apartment building.

I have a simple rule for this:

American servicemen first

Don't worry about the press, the political considerations or what the neighbors are going to say or think. Take a leadership position and accept the responsibility of soldiers lives and accept the fact that I must be willing to commit to the slaughter of anyone who threatens the lives of my team or force. It is our duty to bring all of our personnel back home alive if at all possible.

Currently we are infested with a generation of leaders who are not willing to commit to the slaughter. When American bodies were beaten, drug, abused and put on television after the battle in Somalia in 1993, there was no response. Recently in Iraq, four American bodies were burned, abused, hacked and torn apart and hung as trophies. The American military and leadership response was zero. Great rhetoric spewed from the mouths of our military leadership, but nothing happened. This is because we have raised a generation of political pussies that look at their bosses (not leaders) and shrug their shoulders.

They are more worried about the "political" decision than doing what their guts tell them.

We have the technology now, as we did in 1993 to send a message to these savages that their behavior is not acceptable. But first, you must have the balls to do it. Our leadership in 1993 did not have the guts to do it and it seems that many of our current military leaders have the same problems. We could easily stop this behavior from happening by sending a message that would echo across the world. What really sent this point home to me is that I have fought beside these warriors and I come back to look their family members in the eye when they could not. I would rather kill a thousand booger eaters than have to look another American wife, son or daughter in the eye and tell them how their family member did not make it. The current crop of military leaders are conditioned to think of these as "acceptable loses."

I have never bought into the bull shit theory of acceptable losses. We have the technology, the talent, the aggressiveness and the expertise to bring more of our warriors home than ever before. Our combat, military and political leaders choose to be mediocre at their jobs. That is as simple as I can put it. Were I a general overseeing the recovery of these fine men, I could never sleep well at night knowing that I was such a pussy.

A sample of the thought process can be gleamed through the following example as e-mailed me by a former cadet and now Army Officer. Another newly commissioned second lieutenant reports a similar account from Kosovo:

> **"As you may or may not know, my platoon ended up going up to Mitrovica (Where the French are) attached to the Parachute Infantry Regiment from Bragg. The place is very hot as far as activity. Conditions were very austere as we lived at an old tire factory. My platoon's first mission was to conduct a cordon while the infantry searched buildings (at a college) for weapons in the Serb part of town. At first things were going ok as we started right when the curfew was over in the morning. A couple of Serbs even said that they were glad that we were here. I was also interviewed by Rugger's International News**

Agency and Radio Free Europe. But a couple of hours later, the Search was over and they still had us cordoning off the area because the French were not done. Then some of the Serbs started to get angry because some of us had Albanian interpreters. One interpreter even had to be evacuated from another TCP(Traffic Control Point) that the Anti-Tank Platoon had because they were threatening to kill him.

American troops were not kicking down doors as the Serbs claimed in the news. The United Nations Mission in Kosovo Police apparently had other plans and were kicking down doors. American troops did have people cut locks on doors which made the Serbs angry. Several weapons and a grenade were found. Then all hell broke loose everywhere. Pretty soon we had a mob of over 3000 Serbs that were hurling insults, rocks and bricks at us. We mounted our vehicles and I was waiting for the word to get out of there, because shooting someone would still not have been a good move at that point. I was spit on, my gunner was hit in the K-pot with a rock, another one of the gunners in my platoon broke a finger with a rock, another gunner's tooth was chipped, and the Serbs broke windows and mirrors in our up-armored HMMWVs. We were completely surrounded and I finally told my driver and the squad I was with to go and have the rest of the platoon meet us by the east bridge which crossed back over to the South (Albanian) side.

The Infantry was also attacked, but no one ever fired any weapons at us and we did not see any. The French pretty much let all of this happen, but one French soldier actually pushed Serbs back away from me while I mounted my vehicle. The entire Search element, the AT Platoons, the snipers, and my platoon got back to the tire factory wondering "What the hell just happened to us???"

We literally felt like we had gone into a football game and got our butts kicked. LTC Smith, the BC in charge of us said that we had done our jobs, and we all maintained excellent discipline by not upgrading our level of force to something which would have been an international incident. I felt bad because I had told my gunner to stay up on the gun ready to shoot if the threat possessed itself, right before he got hit in the K-pot.

The following day at dusk, we marched across into the North side of Mitrovica to a neighborhood called Little Bosnia, because of the Serb/Albanian/Turk mix population. These people were much poorer, but the neighborhood was adjacent to the one that we had been attacked in the day prior. My platoon provided a screen for the search element. The whole operation took place without incident, but we had to stop the search, because we had gotten word that up to 40,000 Ethnic Albanians were on their way to Mitrovica from the South. We went back to the tire factory and stood by as we waited for word to move. Over 40,000 Albanians from as far as Pristina had showed up with the intent of returning ethnic Albanians to the North side. They went up to the east bridge which was occupied by a Bradley platoon, some Brits and some French troops which ended up having to use tear gas on the Serbs that had gathered on the North end of the bridge because they felt that the Albanians were coming with weapons and KFOR was not doing anything about it. The Albanian Demonstration was peaceful, however. No one ever came to the East Bridge, which my platoon was occupying with the Germans and the French but the French troops were very nervous and closed off the bridge anyway (Albanians don't like the French because they believe them to be Serb allies). We held the bridge for over 7 hours and again we left with no incident.

The following day my platoon had to provide a presence patrol of an area that was completely bombed out. This area had no inhabitants and looked like what the future looks like in the movie The Terminator. All rubble, buildings barely standing, and streets empty. It was a significant area, because snipers had been reported just across the river on the Serb side.

On the last day, my platoon again provided a screen for the search element, this time in a completely Serb area and this time with less than lethal munitions and riot control gear. This time the plan was once the search was over, my platoon and another MP platoon that had been brought up the day prior, would lead the infantry through any Serb mob and make our way back across the west bridge. This time if they started throwing rocks, we would snatch them up to make an example of them. If they continued to throw rocks, they would be hit my 40mm M203 rubber bullets, foam baton rounds, and multiple foam baton rounds. If that didn't work or if they started shooting because they saw us shooting, we would go to the real stuff... 5.56mm ball and tracer. We really thought that we were going to have to shoot our way out. One concern was that if we started shooting the less than lethal munitions at them, their snipers would see us shooting and Serbs falling, not knowing that we were not shooting real bullets. Their snipers might then start shooting at us and we would have to start shooting real bullets. When the search was finished, not enough of a crowd had gathered and the French were able to hold off the Serbs. We moved back across the bridge standing a little bit more proud,

**because this time we were leaving on our own terms. The Serbs were not able to get things coordinated that day. All they could do was hurl insults at us while we marched by. I am glad that no one had to die or get hurt that day, but I am also disappointed that I did not get to see how a 40mm M203 rubber bullet could knock someone on their ass and make their world hurt.**

**My platoon accomplished the missions it was given, and the soldiers maintained excellent discipline and restraint, preventing any unnecessary loss of life. Keep in mind that not all Serbs feel that way towards Americans. The Serbs in the American Sector actually count on us for their protection. The Serbs in Mitrovica still don't like that we bombed Serbia for 78 days. My platoon may return, and if we do, we are ready to deal with whatever missions we may be given."** (Bubba)

In the narrative, I put the details of the commander's comments not as a personal attack, but as a learning point. I have witnessed this type of behavior happen time and time again throughout my career and it always causes problems. Individuals selected for Special Operations generally have a focused and determined mind-set upon being selected. Without it, they generally would not have made the selection process. Many find religion after their induction and I do not have a problem with that as long as it is kept in its place. I have commented during my combat mindset class that the time to pray is before the battle or after the battle, but during the battle you must focus on killing, the mission is killing the bad guys.

This is where the problem comes in. Military officers should be surgical to a point, but when it comes to the safety and welfare of their troops, they need to draw the line. Should you need more air strikes or artillery, to effectively protect your troops, you should have your mind committed to this prior to the battle. I would urge every soldier to ask their commander a question prior to combat operations, "How many people are you willing to kill to bring us back?" The answers will probably surprise you. As a soldier going into harm's way, you need to known where everyone stands on this issue. If leaders start back peddling on a simple question, they will most certainly do it when times get tough. As a leader, you need to do some serious soul searching and personally establish what price they you are willing to pay to bring your men home.

## TRAINING VS. COMBAT LEADERHSIP

Whether it be an Officer or NCO, if they can't make the hard decisions in peacetime they will find it harder to do it under the stress of combat. Routinely force them to make hard calls during training scenarios so as to visualize and work the solutions out prior to encountering a life and death situation. For example, in Special Operations, we go through thousands of hours of live fire, close quarter combat training, entertaining every possible scenario and adjusting our tactics to simple drills that will handle them all. Why? Referring back to the muscle memory equation, it takes 2000-3000 repetitions to get it down. How about "mental muscle" memory? What do you think the difference is there? Probably not much at all. So, if a shooter on the ground is doing repetition after repetition at their common skills, should a commander being doing the same type of mental rehearsals? You bet. Five or six times in a command bird is inadequate. Leaders need to mentally rehearse the various options that can play out and make the appropriate decisions.

Yes, it would require a bit of work, but no more than we currently do with shoot/don't shoot scenarios on the interactive video training machines. Common combat scenarios could be played out and a common list of options drafted that would give the commander multiple solutions to a problem. Solutions that could be put away for future use in the same type scenarios. Combat can be described in varying degrees or intensities. I have participated in training scenarios that were more intense and difficult tactically intense than many of the real life situations I encountered. Combat takes many forms, but our mindset for it should be limited to one simple mindset.

# BOYD'S LOOP AND
# EFFECTIVE COMBAT LEADERSHIP

The reason we should seek out simple techniques is that if we don't use them, we are setting ourselves up for failure on the battlefield. As technology grows, so does our ability to amass battlefield intelligence. I described earlier that at the team level, I use Boyd's loop to describe how I process information at the individual and team tactical level. The same must be done at the command levels. With so much information being input, commanders need to filter out what is fluff and what is critically important information reference their current tactical situation.

At the team level, I learned to handle one situation at a time and develop a few simple tactical ways to solve the problem. Use the movement to the breach point as an example and generally develop one to two drills that I use on foot to reach the breach point. Each drill would handle four to five common worse case situations that could occur. The same needs to happen at the combat leadership level. Use the infiltration of a group or force into a target area as an example. You should develop one to two simple and effective methods for ground, air or water. These techniques should involve worse case scenarios such as getting shot at and the best way to maneuver your force, mass your fires and neutralize and push through the threat should you be engaged. The military uses air support to augment and aid in infiltrations. Local law enforcement can use snipers as a source of fire support. In either case, it is easier and more efficient to take the ground once, than twice. Also, at the higher levels, you can equate tanks or armored personnel carriers as individuals and several of them as part of a team. All the principles of tactical empowerment still apply to these combat teams.

## KEY POINTS

- ASK YOUR LEADERSHIP A SIMPLE QUESTION BEFORE CONDUCTING COMBAT OPERATIONS, " HOW MANY PEOPLE ARE YOU WILL TO KILL TO GET US OUT?"
- ENSURE RELIGIOUS ISSUES ARE ADDRESSED PRIOR TO COMBAT OPERATIONS (SEE ABOVE QUESTION).
- REMOVE LEADERS WHO CANNOT MAKE THE HARD PEACETIME DECISIONS. THEY WILL FAIL IN COMBAT.

# CHAPTER EIGHT

# TRAINING FOR THE FIGHT

*"Above all, we must realize that no arsenal or no weapon in the arsenals of the world is so formidable as the will and moral courage of free men and women. It is a weapon our adversaries in today's world do not have. It is a weapon that we as Americans do have. Let that be understood by those who practice terrorism and prey upon their neighbors."*

Ronald Reagan

- Levels Of Training And Performance
- The Path Of Success
- Training Responsibilities And Sequence
- Training Pitfalls
- Accelerating The Ooda Loop
- Rehearsals
- After Action Reports/review (Aar's)
- Maintenance Training And Evaluations
- Evaluations

## THE RADIO STATION

It was a near miss. We tried again to pinpoint the target, but with no success. The intel guys would continue to try to provide us with timely and reliable information and we would continue to rehearse. We had not worked with a vehicle assault configuration in years, so we developed a simple plan using some of our security personnel and HUMMVEE's. We were assigned a driver, a Track Commander (TC) and a gunner. The driver's job was simple enough, put the vehicle where we need it. The gunner mission would be as simple, shoot at any bad guys that presented a threat to our force. The TC's job was a bit more difficult. He needed to control the driver, gunner and know exactly where the vehicle was at all times, logging in checkpoints as we drove. Should we make contact, he and his crew would have to act in concert with the other vehicles to ensure that swift and decisive action was taken to get the "hell out of dodge".

Our vehicle's TC, was a good man and we worked well together. We planned out how we were going to load the vehicle and what actions we were going to take on contact. We established fields of fire for every person on the vehicle and made it understood that one side might be in contact with the enemy and the other side must still watch their sector and ensure that the bad guys were not going to hit us from both sides at the same time. This took discipline and focus, as your partner with his back to you might be actively sending rounds down range, so you could not afford to turn around and drop security of your sector. You had to trust he was hitting his target and that the lead and trail vehicles were helping him out with fire from their vehicles.

While waiting for dark to come, we prepared and double checked all our personal gear to include gun lights, markers, personal lights, emergency strobe lights and lasers for our weapons. Once everything was checked and spare batteries were put in the gear, we checked the vehicles out. Sandbags were placed on the floorboards and bed of the vehicles to stop or slow down shrapnel from mines or improvised explosive devices (IED's) placed in the road. We had seen videos of vehicles cut in two because of these homemade improvised mines and they were just as deadly as the ones the military made. We made sure we brought the team break-away-bag, a small rucksack packed with extra ammo, bandages, and water. This was stuff you might need if you had to leave a vehicle should it become disabled. This would also give you a bit more ammo to sustain yourself should you need to stand and fight for a while.

Once the vehicle was checked and double checked, we quietly assembled around it and reviewed any last points prior to our movement time. As the time came for our rehearsal move, the TC and I walked around the vehicle to ensure that all my guys were up, aboard and ready. I then took my spot behind the TC, who was seated in the right front passenger seat. This way I could talk to him almost face to face during the movement. The vehicle TC's gave the ready count to the convoy commander and we began our movement around the camp. We probably drove 10 kilometers that night, allowing the drivers to get used to following other vehicles, keeping pace and maintaining the proper distance. We moved the vehicles into a staging area where we dismounted and conducted a dry run rehearsal on a simulated target. Once this was complete, we got accountability of our teams and forces and then waited by the vehicles in security positions before giving the word to remount.

Once the go ahead was given, I as the team leader, was the last to remount. I needed to see that each of my guys was on the vehicle. I would then pass the word to the vehicle TC, who would again relay the information to the convoy commander. We would then begin our movement. It was critical to ensure that this remounting process was swift and that we began moving again. Speed and movement was our security and none of us liked to be cooped up in a vehicle that you could not effectively maneuver or fight from. One knuckle-head with an AK could put a great deal of effective fire on seven guys stuffed into one HMMWV. Even a bad guy that was not an accomplished a marksman could get lucky and injure or kill one or more soldiers.

We returned back to our staging area and quickly debriefed the actions as a team and then I went to the main debriefing. The plan was coming together and the movement was becoming a bit more polished. The word was passed that if the hit did not go tonight, it would probably go tomorrow night. We decided to do another movement and rehearsal to give all of us a chance to work out any bugs and get our plan down.

The major difference in this plan was that we had switched the teams responsible for assaulting and blocking positions to the give the blocking teams a chance to work on their assaulting skills. Originally, my team's mission was to assault the target building. Now it was to provide a security position for the newly assigned assault force. I thought it would be a much easier job, but things were to get busy on this hit and it was to become a bit more challenging.

As it came to pass, the location of the target was found and pinpointed. Intel and vehicle commanders planned a route to and from the target building and area. They started from our assembly area and passed through a friendly Foreign National armed checkpoint, a place that is routinely dangerous. Passage of friendly lines was always a very dangerous and demanding module taught in Ranger School. Anything could happen, as it was the final line you crossed before you went into Indian country. You could have artillery rain down on you prior to the passage or the enemy could simply attack that area or sector. This was not that big of an issue. But, if the enemy attacked while you were crossing the final friendly point, things could get dicey. You had the choice to continue your mission or to return to friendly lines. The problem is that everyone could be shooting at this time. Friendly forces on the line, bad guys, your people and it could become a mess very quickly, especially at night. Compound this with not speaking the language of the friendly forces who own the checkpoint and you could have a major headache. We left one of our unit members as a liaison with these friendly forces so they would be there on our return and could tell the guys behind the guns who we were.

The mission was planned to occur slightly past midnight. We had a routine day ensuring that everything on our vehicles and our person were checked and double-checked. As the sun set, we tried to get some sleep, but that is almost impossible. Your mind continues to race and as you lay there and try to rest, you review the plan in your head to ensure you have taken all the steps to ensure success. At a predetermined time, we woke everyone so they would have a chance to get some food down, take the final latrine call and generally just wake up and get focused.

The team was ready and we moved to the area of our vehicle. I linked up with the other TL's and met with the assault commander to see if any other intel had come to light. There was none and we returned to our vehicles, mounted up and waited for the departure time. As we waited, the occasional team member might dismount and take time for that last piss. The last thing you wanted to think about when going into combat is the pain of a full bladder when you're in Indian country looking for bad guys. Once we were moving we were not stopping for shit. If you got hit, we would not stop to treat unless were back home safe.

The time came and the signal was given to move out. The lumbering convoy picked up its cruising speed and headed toward the passage of lines. This was uneventful and we did not even stop. Our liaison was there and we rolled on through, lights blacked out and ready to do business. As we moved into the city, it looked like a concrete ghost town. The lead vehicle was reporting a few individuals on the street, most were unaware of our presence until the lead vehicle was right on top of them. They would quickly duck behind a post or tree and wait until we passed. The lead vehicle was equipped with suppressed guns and had the ability to neutralize any threats they encountered. All of the people on the way to the target did not want to play. Evidently, this was the first time a group or unit had ever done any night operations and the locals were probably shell shocked. Most did not know of our presence until we were face to face and they had no time to react. The diesel engines can be extremely quiet if you learned not to rev them and slowly brought them to an intermediate cruising speed. Our flow and movement pace was going all too well when we hit a snag. The lead vehicles ran into a string of concertina that was across the road. This stopped the entire formation. If driven over, concertina wire will wrap around your tires and axles and eventually shred your tires, while dragging the remainder of the roll behind you. Nasty stuff.

The other problem of encountering an obstacle such as this is the possibility that it is covered by fire. This is the perfect way to stop an entire convoy and allow multiple gunmen to reek havoc on a thin-skinned vehicle formation. In addition to gunfire, you could easily put an improvised explosive device all up and down where the lead vehicle was and take out several vehicles with one push of a button. Fortunately it appeared that someone had pulled the razor wire across the road, left it and gone to bed.

As movement continued, code words were given letting us know that we were getting into the target area. As we made our final turn onto the street that contained our target building, we started looking hard for the first intersection on the left. We were to turn down it and travel to the next intersection and set up a blocking position to protect the assault force. Two vehicles in front of us passed our intersection and headed for the next street. I found our intersection that led to our position being blocked by a vehicle. Not some little Fiat or sedan, but a fricking garbage truck. I just shook my head and told the team to dismount. We were going to have to do this the old fashioned way, on foot. I hated to leave our vehicle behind and the heavy weapon mounted on it, but I had no choice. The assault was going to go and we had to get to that intersection to keep people safe. The team moved in pairs and we drifted past one major opening to a ourtyard on our left and passed several closed doors on the right. As we approached our intersection, we set up in the open in buddy teams, each taking a street to their right or left and a street ahead of them. It was quiet for a few moments and then the silence was broken. One of the Black Hawks containing snipers buzzed low, fast and loud about 50 feet over the target and woke everyone up in the neighborhood. Honey, we're home. I was fucking pissed.

It was an exceptionally clean and surreptitious insertion to that point and everyone and their brother woke up. The door opened on the building we had our backs up against on the corner and someone poked their head out. Scott and Tony grabbed a local, threw him down and flex tied him. All of a sudden, I could see heads poking out up and down doorways on both sides of the street. In addition, the assault team had thrown their first distraction device and it echoed throughout the neighborhood. I could see the assault force enter one of the doorways we bypassed moving to our position. A moment or two after the assault teams entered their breach point, a man appeared from the opening across the street from their entry point, turned and started walking my way. As he did, he profiled an AK-47 at his side, the distinctive half moon magazine giving it away. Not having time to report him, I started to sparkle him with my laser. I knew if I were to engage him now, that the bullets would pass through him and go into the blocking position less than 25 meters to his rear. So, I waited. He did not see us and kept walking right toward our position. He continued to walk and then another man came out of the same opening, following the first man's route. As the first man got about 20 feet away, he must have caught sight of our silhouettes. He kept walking straight and tried to pass the AK toward his opposite side away from us. My thought was that he was going to try and make it to the corner and either get away or try and engage us. I could not take the chance of the latter happening, so I held the laser on him center mass and waited until he was perpendicular to me about 20 feet or away. This would ensure the rounds going through him would impact the wall directly behind him. Correcting for the offset of my laser, I began to engage him with some 5.56 tracer. I watched as the tracer rounds went through him, hit the wall and bounced off. In my mind I stopped with a double tap, firing the two shots that I had always been trained to do. The problem was that he was still standing. This probably only lasted half a second in my mind before I continued firing with two more rounds at which point he fell backward into the stream of bullets. I started to close on him and to my amazement, he stood back up for about a second and then collapsed back down on his back.

I began to scan back down the street for the number two man who had been following, but he was now assholes and elbows running back through the hole where he came. I quickly grabbed a flash bang and threw it hard over the courtyard wall in his direction to let him know that I knew he was there. Turning my attention to the man down, I told Kim to grab the AK and to cover out while I checked him. I knew in my mind that he was dead because my weapon was zeroed and I could never miss at that range. The man was attempting to breathe and he did not appear to be getting oxygen. I soon found out why. Searching him, I found that his jacket on his left side where the bullets had exited, was heavy and full of blood. He was fighting for air, but could not get any. I almost felt sorry for him as I cupped his head with my left hand while I searched him with my right. His eyes rolled back and expired on me.

Up to this point, I had blown two team SOP's in dealing with this bad guy. As a team leader, I should have made Kim put hands on while I covered and I should have flex tied the bad guy prior to searching. I got lucky. During my search I found one of those key chain noise makers that sounds like a star trek phaser. The label on it said Echo-1. This was my team designation, "E" team and this was my designation on the team, E-1. I thought this is fucking spooky and I left it on his body. I thought for a moment about dragging him down the street and throwing his body on the hood of our vehicle, similar to that of a deer, but I figured that it would not look good if someone got shot dragging him back and that the driver would probably have a hard time seeing over him. We got the word to remount, so Kim brought the AK with him and we moved back down the street to our vehicle.

Our order to remount vehicles was a bit premature. The assault teams were still doing business on the inside. I grabbed Kim with his M203 grenade launcher and headed about ten yards back down the alley. I found a dirt pile on the left hand side and we took up a cover position there. I figured that Kim could put some high explosive rounds on the intersection where we left the bad guy. When Pete came out with his team, he looked right and could see the body in the street I had left and no blocking team. I think he also realized that we had already been pulled back. Quickly, he brought his guys down our street and to his vehicle. Soon we were uploaded and we were moving.

Tension was high as the bad guys in the area knew now where we were working. We were all watching our sectors when the vehicle behind us spotted some bad guys in an alley getting ready to light us up. A team member from another vehicle engaged them with a Squad Automatic Weapon (SAW) and made them dance a bit. Scott was also able to put some fire on them before we moved out of sight and range. Our air cover started to work over an area with rockets and mini-guns, which made us feel better. The problem now was getting back through friendly lines without getting shot by friendly or enemy fire during the process. To my relief and amazement, we breezed through without incident. We dismounted our vehicles and I did an inspection and debrief and told Kim to turn the AK over to supply. I wanted to ensure that the weapon was properly processed so I had some physical evidence as to my reason for firing. The command debrief went well and we were able to catch a few hours of sleep.......

## AFTER ACTION COMMENTS

### Sustain:

- Continue aggressive rehearsals

### Improve:

- Individual searching and flex-tying
- Perimeter collapse procedures

## LEVELS OF PERFORMANCE AND TRAINING

While serving in Special Operations, I was able to work with a host of instructors from various tactical units foreign and domestic, large and small. I quickly learned that levels of performance and training vary from organization to organization and unit to unit. Through the years, I had the opportunity to observe training and exercises at all levels ranging from small town teams to foreign national counter-terrorist units. Individual, team and organization level performance and capabilities were directly tied to exceptional leadership. The common thread that ensured exceptional training, was an exceptional cadre responsible for the training. How do you get there? You invest. By investing quality people in training programs and ensuring that they have the resources to pass the needed information down.

A problem area that needs to be addressed that pertains to training is one that I term "poisoning the well." This describes the trend where training sections, organizations and academies are used as depositories for unwanted or substandard individuals. If I were a new police officer reporting to the academy, my initial view or perception of an organization would be greatly shaped by the training cadre. If I saw a group of fat, sloppy, unhappy staff that could not get along, were unprofessional, did not believe in the organization or were dissatisfied with their job assignment, I would soon develop a skewed or tainted view of the organization myself. This would be especially true if I had to spend three to six months working closely with the same staff. I have witnessed overweight, no, overweight is a kind term, better yet, fat instructors, bellies hanging halfway to their knees, screaming at cadets to do more push-up. These worthless, hypocritical living examples of a piss-poor instructor do nothing but expose a double-standard in the chain of command. Cadets can easily see that there is no physical standard in place and that the department lacks any leadership in place to correct it.

I was fortunate to have served with a crew of instructors that set the standard. While in Special Ops, the command supported the selection process and assignment of proven instructors to our training section. It was an incredible experience. Potential instructors were selected from individuals who had successful team leader time under their belts. During my tour as an instructor, my fellow cadre members had combat experience. As a new instructor, you were paired up with another instructor and worked with them while they taught their assigned blocks of instruction. As an instructor rotated out, the new instructor became the primary instructor for that block of instruction and had the latitude to change or improve the material. I noted that every instructor made changes without guidance. They made their presentations and training a little better for the new instructor who would take over the class. This created an exceptional work environment of a cadre seeking perfection in their duties. It also created a united cadre that supported each other, a perception that was readily observed by the students. There were no "chinks in our armor" and the students knew it. The students quickly received the message that they were there to train and not bullshit around. They had a cadre of proven professionals who would put the same gear on and do the same physical events as they would, setting a training standard and system that I still employ today. No one complained or even thought about complaining. Some of these instructor were 15-20 years the senior of their students. I remember when I was going through training and the cadre took us on a seven-mile run carrying an M14 and combat loaded LCE. Our instructors were there right beside us the entire way, enjoying the North Carolina summer heat.

What level or goal should you expect your team to attain? This will differ from group to group. Training time, facilities and equipment plays an important role in this equation. Of course, safety should also be a primary concern and should focus on not injuring a student through negligence or stupidity. Special Operations units, the ones that do business and train on a daily basis might have a standard where they are able to conduct a live fire, multi-breach point, explosive breach mission on a target with an unknown floor plan, where live role players are present. Some will say that it is impossible to do, but, it has been done before. You must be at the top of your game to do it, but it can be safely accomplished with the proper training and safety measures in place. How do they get to such a level? Simple. Hard work and thousands of hours of rehearsals coupled with an outstanding training staff.

## THE PATH OF SUCCESS

Individual skills and tactics must go from what is termed dry-fire or practice, to range fire, to paintball scenarios or simunitions with live role players to combat on the street with little or no changes. This philosophy of "linear progression" will enable you to have a valid system of training that will ensure you climb the tactical ladder safely, quickly and efficiently, helping to ensure mission success. This training philosophy targets the lowest level of the organization, or what I refer to as the "Gumby" level. The Gumby, the man going in the door first, making life and death decisions, should be a primary focus of the training. He is on the tip of the spear and is responsible for the outcome of the operation. If he shoots a hostage by mistake or a friendly officer, it can mean mission failure for the organization as the rest of the unit will be all painted with the same brush of failure. It is our job as leaders and professional trainers to ensure his training and system is safe, simple, efficient and life saving. Implementing complex, confusing and unrealistic systems of shooting and close quarter battle techniques that are not easy to learn and practice are not helping him in his journey towards consistency.

As a trainer and a leader you should look at simplifying the process at every available opportunity.  This should begin with tactics and missions.  Generally law enforcement tactical teams are assigned the big four:

- Hostage Rescue
- High Risk Warrant
- Search Warrant
- Barricade Person

Adding dynamic and slow clearing techniques adds more to your training plate and you will soon realize that you have a full training plate.  The key to developing simple tactics for all these missions is **not to**.  You should instead, focus on developing simple drills or a system that will apply to all the missions with minor changes.  The reason is simple, since trying to develop a different set of drills that will apply to each specific mission is too much information for the individual to try and process.  Further, you will never have the training time needed to become proficient at these drills.  To add, the drills should not be directed at the experienced team leader, but rather at the newest and lowest member of the team.  Trying to memorize too many drills will only confuse and complicate matters resulting in inefficient and bastardized techniques.  Keep it simple.

I like to ask tactical officers in class, what is the difference between getting shot at on a hostage rescue, a high-risk warrant, a search warrant and a barricaded person mission?  The answer is none.  They are all the same, your still getting shot at.  So why have four or five drills when one or two will solve all your problems on all missions.  This is where a good trainer will come in and help keep it simple.  A quality trainer should be able to give you a simple drill or two to handle all the contingencies for a particular problem.  The key is to break down the training into blocks or modules.

For example, I break down targets into five distinct phases for training and work on them as individual modules at first.  They are:

- Movement to the Breach Point
- Breach Points
- Hallways and "T" intersections
- Close Quarter Battle (CQB)
- Consolidation and Reorganization

Teams first work on developing drills to handle all the contingencies that can come up during one module. Using the Movement to the Breach Point example, I teach a drill that will allow the team to handle the following problems:

- Runner
- Complaint with a Gun
- Suspect verbally challenging with a gun on the ground
- Shooter
- Shooter with and officer down

I first talk about the problem of moving to a breach point and all the contingencies that can happen. I then show them a drill that will safely handle all the above problems. I allow the team an hour or two to conduct dry runs with a role player and get the movement and mechanics worked out. I then have the team load up with simunitions and I pre-stage the team around a corner. I then brief my role player on which scenario I want them to play out. The team is signaled and the role player acts out his role. During one scenario the role player will run, in another they will just shoot, in another they will run, in another they will be a compliant person with a gun. Each run is recorded on video and five scenarios are run back to back. A short after action follows after each run and major points are addressed.

The film is reviewed in a classroom environment the next morning when everyone is fresh. Everyone looks at it at normal speed and then if we have something that catches our eye, we rewind and slow it down. We pick it apart for safety, tactical sanity if you will, and the effectiveness of massing fires on the bad guy. We also ask the role player for his input as to what they saw. Were they mentally and visually overwhelmed? Was the amount and accuracy of the fire sufficient to neutralize them. Once we look at all the video and hash out all the questions or problems and if the tactic is agreed upon, we go do it again and reinforce it. Taking it a step further, once the drill is mastered with simmunitions or paintball, it can then be practiced on a flat live fire range under controlled supervision. Team leaders can then run their team through dry and then by giving one person on the team ammunition and checking the hits after each run. You can build up to everyone live firing once the team has demonstrated proper safety and accuracy habits.

I believe that certain skills and training should be deferred to the individual level for maintenance and should not need supervision when performing. Shooting and physical training are two of these. With availability of weapons, ammunition and ranges, individuals should take their own initiative to practice their shooting skills. As a team leader, I do not want to waste my precious one day a month of training, standing over my guys on a flat range. They should be able to dry-fire at night at home in their garage and then live fire on their own time. I will spot check them with team drills every few months and conduct bi-annual evaluations. The same goes for physical training. This is an individual responsibility and we may go for a team run before training on training days just to keep everyone honest. On collective training days, team drills and collective training are the priority.

## TRAINING RESPONSIBILITIES AND SEQUENCE

Leadership at the team and organizational level must be knowledgeable about safety, tactics and techniques to ensure training and mission success. Too many times our leaders are required to be "administrators" and are not savvy as to what the troops are doing and why. This is evident by the number of training accidents which occur as a result of the training officers being directly responsible for the fatal or near fatal incidents. Routinely these leaders are unchained from their desks, torn from their computers and designated as safety officers. They have little or no concept of the safety requirements of the tactical training they are hosting or what can happen.

In my three years as a law enforcement trainer, I have kept abreast of training accidents at the individual, team and organizational level. When I started my training business, more tactical law enforcement officers were killed in my state by a string of friendly fire shootings or by "accident", than by bad guys. It was incredible. The typical organizational solution to the problem was to spend more money on training equipment, i.e. simunition weapons instead of taking a hard look at safety and training practices. This number has significantly decreased, but from time to time you hear of officers screwing around resulting in an exceptional officer or friend tragically bang shot and killed. This does not need to happen, yet it does.

As a soldier or law enforcement officer, you have the choice to be good at what you do, or to be lucky. I choose to be good. If you choose to be lucky (sloppy), the law of averages will get you. And it will not get only you. The entire team and department will suffer. A recent friendly fire incident on a major tactical team during a real life situation resulted in the loss of five officers. The officer that was shot, was permanently crippled and is working in an administrative division. The officer that fired the shot and the team leader who was in charge of the team are also off the tactical team. Two others left as part of their action or inaction during the incident. Five lost and not to mention the outstanding career and life diverted by the officer being shot. This all resulted from violating one simple safety rule. I will not even mention the morale and litigation problems that will arise from this. It is a waste. Where can we point the blame? The individual, team and organization are responsible.

At the individual level, the officer firing a shot violated a basic safety rule, "Lead shooter has priority of shot," which means that if you're in the back of the stack, or have officers in front of you, you can't shoot. You have to move on line with those officers or in front of them to safely make the required shot. You will get lucky four out of five times and get away with it, but the fifth time you will tag your partner. As a former action guy, I would always be situationally aware of soldiers around me, their weapon and safety posture, because they can kill you just as dead as a bad guy. If someone did something unsafe, I would correct them on the spot.

At the team level, the team leader needs to ensure the team was trained up to the required levels to successfully complete the mission. This is where the team leader needs to monitor team drills and ensure that everyone is adhering to the safety rules while in training. The team leader also has to have the guts to correct team members when they see them violating safety rules.. Failure to do so will ingrain poor habits that will transfer to live operations. Taking it a step further to the organizational level, these leaders did not spot check training to ensure that the team leaders and members were following the proper safety guidelines and enforcing proper safety practices.

As a leader, the choice is yours. Invest in training with quality trainers or poison your well. What would you want to see as a new student, a combat proven leader or a "left over" or screw up who has no experience? Our business is too dangerous not to pass the right knowledge down by the proper instructors. Amateurs will only create an unsafe working environment. Further, ensure your individual training compliments your team training. Ensure your team training compliments the organizational training. Hold team leaders accountable for both. Give them the time, assets and personnel to do the job and then hold them accountable.

## TRAINING PITFALLS

Awareness of a trap is the first step in its avoidance. With that thought, failure to maximize training time is a common complaint and issue in the tactical field. It is critical to use your training time efficiently. I see teams that have one or two training days a month. The key to using this allocated time is to ensure you training day is planned, rehearsed and ready to go with trainers, equipment and locations. Some teams fall into the trap of the social training day. They come late, take a long lunch and then leave early feeling that they have accomplished their goals. They are sadly mistaken.

Units that fall into this trap will eventually be compromised on a mission and will wonder what happened. If you do not take the training seriously or are not willing to commit time and resources, you're probably better off disbanding your team until you do. Some tactical teams members are of the mind that unless they are getting the time either comped or off, they will not go to training. They feel by simply being issued the special gear, they are qualified to do the mission. An old instructor said to me, "It takes five minutes to dress like a commando, but years to become one." This attitude of the "the gear makes me," is false. You always make the gear.

Another pitfall is the team leader who sends their tactical personnel to every bit of training that comes up, but on their return, they fail to develop any consistent tactics or SOP's. Generally, tactical officers are the type "A" personalities who love to sharp shoot and argue with each other. When an officer attends a training course, generally they can absorb only 50 percent of the material that they are exposed to. Most often they loose the finer points. When they complete the course and bring this information back, it becomes a "cat fight" of sorts to relay this information to the team. Old members will say, "that's bullshit," we tried that ten years ago, etc. You find that tactics are like assholes, everyone has one and they want to show it to you. Generally, unless it is an open-minded team and team leader, much of the information is suppressed and not tried. Or, the common response is that we will talk about it for a month and bring it up at the next training meeting. People forget or they move on to a new block of training and never do get back to it.

Other teams have vocal dominant members who come back from training pushing a technique that they have just learned and it becomes law. This is done even though they have never used it with simunitions, video or in live fire, to verify if it is valid. Some leaders implement the latest fad technique without properly researching it. These new techniques will generally work dry, but throw in role players and simunitons, the problems jump out at you.

Still others implement the latest and greatest technique just because the instructor was from this or that organization. This can be dangerous for several reasons. First, there are a slew of instructors who are one-time wonders out in the community. One type of instructor is the trainer who has been to all the schools and their walls are covered by certificates, but have never kicked in a door on an actual mission. The problem here is the schoolbook answer, versus the reality, tried and tested answer. As a friend once said, an instructor who has done only homework with no fieldwork will make a questionable instructor. Schoolwork must be accompanied by fieldwork.

Another type of instructor is the one who went to a tactical unit for a short time and was "purged" shortly thereafter. But because he was there, they now wear the badge of authority because they spent a year in that unit while on probation the entire time. They may be hailed as a subject matter expert. Many times these individuals were flushed out for a reason such as an injury, technical incompetence or a consistent personality conflict. I can deal with instructors who left because of injuries. Special Operations and law enforcement tactical operations is a fast moving game where you can easily be injured in training or on the job during a mission. Instead of pushing these types of individuals out of the arena, we should use them and glean as much information as we can from them. The military can easily put them into training committees and law enforcement can assign them to training academies. The individuals in question may hate the idea of this, but I hate to see their talent and knowledge leave the organization. Training groups and academies are a great place to rehab as they routinely have an eight to five schedule and gym facilities are usually available.

## REHEARSALS

Rehearsals are the life-blood of a successful mission. This is not a fancy statement, but it is simple and true. As a private in the Army, I honestly could not see the big picture of why rehearsals were important until I went to Special Operations. The reason was because I was at the Gumby level and not well informed. I was loaded down with equipment and told to march here or there and take instructions once I arrived. The other reason for my lack of understanding was that we generally did poor rehearsals. As I would learn later in life, you need to maximize your rehearsal time, whether they be dry, or wet, because your life depends on it. Dry rehearsals are generally conducted without live ammunition, where wet rehearsals usually include live fire training.

We discussed returning from a school or course with new tactical drills. These drills need to be validated before they are accepted as gospel. How do we accomplish this? We use all the tools in our training arsenal. Tools such as simunition, air soft or paintball weapons can provide valuable feedback. We now have the ability to replicate getting shot at and this adds a mathematical probability to our training. The probability deals with a ratio of hits from the bad guy while performing a certain drill or movement. Simply run your battle or tactic with a live roll player who will shoot back. Run the same drill several times back-to-back and video the training. Between runs, count how many hits the bad guy was able to deliver and how many the good guys are able to deliver. Keep a record of this and then try another drill or tactic and keep the same statistics. Now review the video. First, look for a more aggressive system that masses your fires or lets everyone safely shoot. The tactic should also get everyone out of the kill zone during the contact. And finally, the drill or tactics should be safe and simple to remember. While reviewing the video, check the real time speed of the drill and which drill gives you a higher hit ratio than the bad guy. Your tactic should give you a 4:1 or 5:1 hit ratio to be considered valid. Yes, officers can get shot, and will. This is the nature of the beast. This is also why we wear all the Kevlar and protective gear and carry guns. Further, I will tell you out of experience that the more bullets you can put into a bad guy, the faster they die. So whenever possible, safely mass your fire and make the threats go away sooner.

The added benefit of the training is the mental conditioning it will enable the individual to develop. Your personnel should train to bring all the critical marksmanship skills to bear at one critical moment, seeing your front sight on the target and squeeze. This simple act is what I term a fine motor skill and it must be ingrained in your psyche. Force on force training will help you accomplish it when you train to do it. Using the above weapon systems, you can hold your personnel accountable for accuracy and lost rounds. You can also see where these lost rounds go and understand why it is important to make surgical shots.

In addition, students can now mentally condition themselves to fire and continue to fight, even thought they have been hit. This important mindset of "fighting through" became very obvious to me during intense combat operations. I have watched soldiers and leaders who were hit, with minor non-life threatening wounds, mentally shut down and give up, while they still had the means to fight. This was not their fault, but rather a training failure. While migrating through my service career, it was customary that while conducting battle drills, when you got hit, you stop. At the time, MILES gear was the rage and when your nodule recorded a hit with a laser and your beeper went off, you were required to stop in your tracks. This only compounded and reinforced the mental "quit when your hit" attitude. We conditioned a generation and an Army to stop when you're hit, no matter the severity of the wound. I witnessed numerous soldiers who could have stayed in the fight, but mentally shut down and quit because of their prior erroneous training.

I inform students of this in my current training and tell them not to go down or quit unless I put you down. I advise students that if even if the simmuniton or paintball round strikes them right between the eyes, don't quit. Wipe it away and fight through, neutralize the enemy.

Start the mental programming necessary for their survival during their current training. If I do have students that mentally give up, I require the team to carry them off target as a punishment. Generally, students only give up one time and their team talks to them about their mindset as they are hauled out of the building.

This brings to mind another law enforcement raid that the officers were lucky that the bad guy did not have a fight through mindset. This tactical team was forced by an apartment being located upstairs to enter a single breach point. This is a dangerous situation. It forces all the officers into one cone of fire for a brief second or two before flooding in and clearing the threat area.

The assault was initiated by a distraction device which was detonated on a "bang pole," outside the apartment bedroom window. The entry team entered the front door and rapidly took an armed bad guy down who was sitting in a chair in the living room area. They then proceeded to the bedroom area to finish securing the apartment. Well, the other bad guy was in the bedroom with his girlfriend when the device went off and he positioned himself behind the bed, covering down on the door with a 1911 .45 pistol. As officers entered the room he began shooting. He struck the number one man twice, once in the wrist and once in the head. They bullet went through the officers goggles, entered his head above his eye. The bullet then traveled under the scalp and around the officer's head, exiting the back. The officer, knowing he was hit, called it out. His partner, grabbed him and drug him into a nearby bathroom. A third officer entered the room and found that bad guy had fired the seven rounds in the magazine, threw down the weapon on the bed and put his hands up, using his girlfriend as a shield. He was then taken into custody.

The problem I have was that that the threat was not neutralized. Had the offender had a high capacity magazine or a rifle with a 30 round magazine, the story might be much different. The officer who was shot, later recalled that it was like getting hit with a sledge hammer. The actions of his partner, rendering aid first, was a conditioned response. I have always believed in the opposite, "one dead body does not justify two." You must learn to ignore the dead and injured and concentrate on neutralizing the threat or you will have more dead and wounded.

These officers were fortunate and the situation could have resulted in a more serious encounter.

# AFTER ACTION REPORT/REVIEW (AAR'S)

After Action Review/Report (AAR's) are critical to extracting lessons learned and ensuring that honesty, integrity and candor are always held to a high standard within the force. Two types of AAR's that come to mind are the informal debriefings that occur after a mission with either the key leaders or the entire group. The other is the formal AAR's that consists of detailed written lessons learned that are passed through the chain of command for their information and to other units that may be going into harm's way. These units can use well written AAR's to adjust their training or to develop new and innovative training plans to deal with the problems or situations that were encountered.

Routinely the informal AAR process is used during training and rehearsals to quickly identify problem areas and develop solutions. For example, your element is tasked with a mission to raid a walled compound in a small village. You develop a plan and find another small empty village about the same size and shape to do your rehearsals on. You begin your rehearsals with your company consisting of three maneuver platoons and a headquarters platoon. You task one platoon to block or seal the compound while the other two platoons assault. You run your dry rehearsal without roll players on the target and go through your entire plan, movement, actions on and during the assault, consolidation and then exfiltration from the target. All your platoons report back to your assembly area or staging area from where you started. You need now to elicit information that will be critical to make the next rehearsal even smoother.

You can gather every person in the company together or you can bring in key leaders to the AAR. Since your probably going to do further rehearsals, the troops probably need to clean and adjust gear, further prepare their vehicles, up load ammo, etc. While they are doing this, the key leaders can be sorting out what happened and how to fix it. First, I would ensure that all squad leaders, platoon sergeants and platoon leaders are present. I would then start by briefing the overall concept of the mission and then ask for the key element leaders to describe what they saw, what problems they encountered and a solution for fixing it. The key to successful briefings are to keep them professional, sterile and not allow finger pointing. If someone screws up, it will be obvious to everyone. You want to create an atmosphere where elements are encouraged to bring up the problems that they encountered and how to fix them, so others may not run into the same problem. Fix it one time, the first time.

Generally, I will start with my lead elements and have them brief major issues and not delve into trivial matters. I really don't want to hear about who did what on their squad, unless it had a great impact on the mission. I will leave the squad issues to the squad leader to deal with. I want to know about how the mission flowed and if we can concentrate on the big issues such as the sequence of our infiltration of the target. Assault squad leaders might bring up the issue of a time delay on getting in and on the target with the way the formation is organized. They may suggest that if we send in the assault force to the compound first and then put the blocking positions in second, because critical surprise time will be gained when penetrating the target. This is a good point and if enough of the personnel agree that this is a better solution, we change it. I prefer to let the individuals that are kicking in the door to plan the plan and execute the plan. As a commander, I am there as a safety valve or sanity check. I will look over the their assault plan and ensure that we do not have any fields of fire problems or we are doing something stupid that will get soldiers killed.

Another technique for debriefings is to keep leaders from rambling. This can be done by reviewing two positive points and two areas than need to be improved. This keeps it simple and as a commander, I would focus on fixing two-to-three things with each rehearsal and this will help your planning and rehearsals exponentially. If you have too many key leaders trying to talk or you have the ones that like to hear themselves talk, you will bring out too many trivial issues and you will forget what is important and what is not. Keep it simple, controlled and non-personal. If individuals have personal issues with other leaders, they take it up after the briefing. The key to the informal AAR is to get the information disseminated and back out to the action guys so they can do another rehearsal.

The first informal AAR may take some time if your plan is rough. But as you fix the two to three items with each rehearsal, your actions will smooth out and the AAR's will shorten to probably just a few minutes with little or no input. Again, it is critical for the guys on the ground to get as much time working through their actions as possible.

## MAINTENANCE TRAINING

Maintenance training for a force can take two forms. The first is a yearly check the block training that encompasses all the missions that the unit is required by their charter to perform. The other is when a unit is deployed into a threat area and you have not conducted a mission of any type in some time, generally a week or so. These "refresher missions" will help keep the unit sharp and focused should the call come.

Routinely I read the chat lines where tactical teams complain of being burned out and not having anything to train on. I just shake my head. I will start by using the worse case example of a part time tactical team who has only one and one half days a month to work on their skills. If you break it down into 12 sessions a year, here is a schedule I would propose.

| Month 1 | Hostage Rescue | Team 1 |
| Month 2 | High Risk Warrant | Team 2 |
| Month 3 | Search Warrant | Team 3 |
| Month 4 | Barricaded Person | Team 4 |
| Month 5 | Vehicle Assaults | Team 5 |
| Month 6 | Evals | Command |

I would then repeat this cycle for the next six months as these are the "core" missions a law enforcement tactical team may face. Why repeat the training? Simple, each of these scenarios can be changed to a different venue the next time they train. You can start with an apartment or small house sized target. The next training can encompass a large house or office building. The third cycle can target, office buildings, school, hospitals, etc. I think you get the picture.

# EVALUATIONS

When I walk into an unfamiliar organization to do an evaluation, I keep my evaluation system simple. I am professional, polite, keep my mouth shut and my eyes open. What am I looking for? Everything. First, I look to see how individuals perform at their level and what is their motivation and initiative is like? Next, I look to see if they do things on their own initiative or they have to wait for guidance from above. This will readily indicate the type of leadership style present in the organization. Hopefully it is an empowerment to the lowest level. If not, it will probably be a tightly controlled authoritarian or near dictatorship. Also, I look at their individual skills, such as weapon safety and how they handle their firearms and their load, unload and clearing procedures. Is it safe, do they have a system for safety and are they conscious of it?

I then watch the team leaders and see how they are performing. Do they spot check and pass information as it becomes available. Does the team have a scripted system of doing business or is the team leader having to point out every detail to team members. Is there an assistant team leader present ensuring accountability for the team and their equipment, freeing up the team leader to begin planning.

Observing the command staff, I look to see if they are organized and efficient and that information freely flows to the team level. Do leaders come in and take charge or do they wait for key personnel, the "old reliable," to come in and make it happen? I watched this happen with a great organization on a large exercise. Key personnel that routinely took charge, intentionally delayed their arrival to the crisis area to see what their subordinates would do. In this case, their subordinates were so conditioned to their leaders being their, giving direction and guidance that they waited, and waited and waited... All the while the scenarios were still playing out on the target, as they do in real life. It was a great learning experience for everyone.

Back to training evaluations. Looking at the training and tactical scenarios that an organization sets up for their team will provide you with an accurate snapshot of the importance and professionalism of the entire command staff. If the staff puts a great deal of work and thought into scenarios, it is a good indicator that the organization takes the training seriously.

Routinely I am asked by individuals and units that I train, how do we stack up? To give an honest evaluation of a tactical unit, you must first know what is at both ends of the spectrum so to speak. Using the "yardstick" analogy, I was able to see organizations from all over the world operate and I would have to use my base of reference to determine their level of performance.

This may seem like a simple task, but it is dependant on several variables of the tactical organization. You must first look at the unit's mission or missions and determine if they have the numbers to do the job. Smaller departments sometimes have tactical teams whose numbers barely reaches into the double digits. Conducting a complex multi-breach point hostage rescue operation generally requires twice that number of personnel. If that team has not worked out a mutual aid agreement with another agency, they may lack the personnel to properly do the job. Of course, they may execute the mission anyway and be lucky, but we should not rely on luck in this business.

Next, available personnel for selection can be a critical component for a tactical team. If the host department only has 25 sworn personnel and ten are on the tactical team, you may wonder about their capabilities. On the other hand, I have witnessed departments with thousands of officers where the management did not care for tactical units and they deliberately kept them undermanned. What key components have a direct effect on both these issues? Leadership and conviction. I have witnessed small departments that could not afford the overtime, but the guys on the team used their own time and money to ensure they had the proper gear and that conducted enough training to sustain themselves and to properly execute a mission. This not only shows heart, but incredible conviction to the mission.

## KEY POINTS

- TRAIN AS YOU FIGHT
- VALIDATE ALL TACTICS AND DRILL PRIOR TO COMBAT
- USE VIDEO WHENEVER POSSIBLE FOR AAR'S
- ENSURE AAR'S ARE HONEST AND PROMOTE CANDOR. THEY SHOULD FOCUS ON SOLVING THE PROBLEMS AND NOT POINT FINGERS

CHAPTER NINE

# LEADERSHIP PLANNING

*"Never tell people how to do things. Tell them what to do and they will surprise you with their ingenuity.*

George Patton

- Your Planning System
- One Or Many Planners, What Serves You Best
- Rehearse Your Planning Sessions
- Empower Your Leadership
- The Quickest And Most Efficient Way To Plan

## THE MISSION

We received another intel hit from a "reliable" source that our priority target was spotted in a vehicle and had been driven to a residential house. The team leaders quickly dressed, secured their weapons and reported to the TOC. The information was simple and straight forward. The "big" man on our target list was spotted by U.S. Forces leaving a foreign embassy. The forces notified our assets and eyes were put on the vehicle. The vehicle entered a walled compound that was located in an upscale portion of the city. We checked the imagery and found that there were two to three vehicles present in the compound. As the forces assembled, a new assault commander was rotated in to perform the command and control responsibilities as the group leader. This particular leader had been on other hits and watched the planning process, but had

150

never actually performed the job before on a real mission. As we gathered around the dry erase board in the TOC, the commander grabbed a dry erase pen and decided he was going to take charge and designate how the assault was going to go down. As team leaders, we just sat back and watched.

He had been programmed through his leadership training that he was to take charge from the front and lead. What he found as he watched our hasty planning session was that with the amount of assault, support, and cover aircraft in our package, that there was too much information for him to process quickly. He looked at the sketch of the target for a moment and realized he was in over his head. He handed the dry erase pen to a sergeant major and turned over the planning phase to the tactical element leaders. The assault team leaders looked at the sketch and let the lead team pick the point of insertion where we could get our four packages in. The assault pilots also looked at the plan with them to ensure the area was large enough to get the bird in. Then, the security guys came up and picked out the best positions to set their blocking forces in with their pilots. The gun pilots sat back and watched both, figuring the best plan of attack to ensure that they could provide the best cover should we encounter threats. It was done, in two to three minutes and we had a plan to integrate assault, cover and attack aircraft into one simple template plan. We moved out to our birds, briefed our team members and our individual pilots to ensure we would be landing according to the plan. We then mounted up on our birds and waited for the lift off signal.

This run would be fast, almost a straight line run into the target. Blades were turning and we began pushing air and started our move. The initial snake like formation was inbound, hot and moving with a purpose. We got the one-minute from the pilot and unhooked our safety lines. The attack birds did not pick up any threats and screamed past their targets. We were hot on their ass. We were scanning hard on our final approach and our pilot picked up a wire in our path at the last minute and had to do a near vertical insertion. He smoothly set down and we broke to the right side of the bird. We were faced with a compound wall with two heavy metal gates to our front. On our left was a small corner snack stand that jutted out off the main wall, one to two meters deep.

We ported the window with our weapons to ensure it was clear of potential threats and refocused our attention on the gates. Team breachers were already placing charges on the gates and we were looking for places to hide from the impending blast. They gave the blast signal "fire in the hole" and we braced for the shock of the charge. Heavy metal gates required a somewhat larger charge with the old military "P" for plenty of explosives factored in. The charges blew and it rocked us a bit, but we were used to it by now. We would get ninety degrees off the blast plane and keep our mouth open so as not to overpressure the lungs. We were probably only 15-20 feet from the point of detonation, but the 90 degree factor and the heavy walls helped protect us.

The sharp crack coupled with the dust clouds and debris that blew past us let us know the charges had gone off. We moved in and entered the gate to the right, as the gate on the left was not yet open. We moved down a long driveway in a modified wedge and focused on the house to our right. Remembering what the target looked like in the planning session, I knew we were at the wrong house. Our photos showed two mirror houses, one on the right and one left. We were approaching the right one and our target was over the wall to our left. Looking left, I saw a doorway in the compound wall and knew it had to lead to the right house. I told the team to move left. As we punched through the gate, we crossed a short patio and entered a dining room with a table full of hot spaghetti fit for a king. We started to clear and began to put everyone down. We quickly took the dining room and kitchen down and then moved down the hall to the living areas. A 30 foot hallway with two doors right and a door left ended with a far door that led outside. We put a woman down in the hallway coming out of a room on the left. We cleared the first room on our right and then a door slammed shut on next room down. It made the hair stand up as we pushed down the hallway. Focusing on the slammed door on our right, we covered it while we cleared the room the woman had come out of. When the team gave a verbal clear, I told my breacher to "charge it." I grabbed the woman by the hand who was laying on the floor and drug her back down the hallway around a corner where she would be safe from the blast. I moved down the hall and took up a position in the room across from the charge. My breacher called burning and pulled back into our room. The charge went off and we moved through the smoke and cleared the room. It was empty and it appeared that the wind had blown the door shut. We came back out and cleared through the door at the end off the hallway only to link up with a team who was pinning the rear of the compound.

Moving back in, we started to consolidate all the personnel on the target into the living room area. The men were placed on one side, women on the other. Looking over the men, I knew what had happened. We had a look alike, a person that looked like our target, but this guy was much older and fatter. Our intel sources had mistaken this person for our target and we thought it was better to take action than to kick ourselves later for not taking action. We handed over our prisoners to the teams designated to further search, control and move them. Reporting to the assault commander that I had all my personnel, we prepared for exfiltration.

## AFTER ACTION COMMENTS

### Sustain:

- Stay alert and stay in the fight. If you're not where you are supposed to be, move to or fight your way to where you need to be. Always look and assess.

### Improve:

- If it is not broke, don't fix it. If the planning sessions you are using are successful and work, keep using them.

## YOUR PLANNING SYSTEM

The planning system you choose should be generic, flexible and fast. It should incorporate all the talent and leadership assets at your disposal. The same system should be practiced and rehearsed during all your training sessions to enable you and your sub unit leaders to refine and streamline their portion of the planning process. Further, the planning staff should be geared to support you and your mission and not dictate policy or tactical guidance to you. Their job is to facilitate the information flow and tactical assets to you and your men. This information should be both verbal and posted.

## ONE OR MANY PLANNERS, WHAT SERVES YOU BEST

I have witnessed just about every type of rapid or deliberate planning session over my military and civilian career and the one that I have seen work the fastest and most efficient in a high stress environment is "collective planning." This session is where all tactical, maneuver and support leaders are present to ensure the plan is understood and well represented. These are the people who are going to kick the doors (assaulters) in, the people who are going to get them close to the doors (pilots/drivers) and the people who are going to protect them from the outside (support), once they are in the target.

Who begins the planning process? The commander should immediately by giving an overall mission statement, then hand the process over to the elements who will next determine the priority of infiltration. For example, if you intend to put your assaulter on the target first, the assault team leaders should take the lead in developing the insertion plan with the pilots or drivers right by their sides to ensure that you can get the air assets or vehicles into where the team leader wants them. The drivers or pilots may say, my vehicle will not fit and cause you to adjust your plan. You want this to take place at the planning board and not on the ground or on final approach while you are taking fire.

Once the assaulters get their plan down, the security force then needs to figure out where they can best protect and serve you. They should conduct planning with their delivery personnel, either pilots or drivers. Assaulters should be looking at this area and ensure they know where their protection is for both their fields of fire or incoming hostile fire. For example, putting a security position too close to you will cause you a headache. When the enemy engages the security position, the rounds that miss the security element will bleed over into your position. Ensure you have cover between you and your security elements.

Once everybody understands the plan and there are no questions or changes, you move out and brief your men. Using a simple sketch map, you point out where you are going and if you can't get in into your primary infiltration point, where your alternate is and how to get there. The pilots or drivers must also confirm these locations. If there are no questions, you are ready to do business.

## REHEARSE YOUR PLANNING SESSIONS

Planning staffs should be required to be at routine training to ensure they have a system that best supports the men going into harm's way. The planning and briefing area should be set-up as it appears in combat to ensure the most efficient system has been implemented. The "staff" and "intel" personnel should be present to feed information to the end user in a quick and efficient manner as they would in a real combat mission. Only by requiring them to participate in routine training will you ensure that they are able to perform these critical tasks. Many times commanders allow the requirement of the day-to-day unit business as an excuse not to attend training. This excuse may fly once in a while, but commanders should ensure they are there and their system is in place. Remember, these intel and planning personnel are generally working in a warm and dry environment when the action guys are freezing, baking or getting pissed on with rain. The least they can do is to work a few more hours in a controlled environment to ensure their area of responsibility is functionally intact.

Rehearsals should include the entire process of alert and notification for a mission as well as deployment of an advance team if required to include a reception of the main force. The planning process should then integrate the entire package through the actual assault or follow on assaults. This may be a one, two or three day process. After Action Reviews (AAR's) should be conducted to ensure that the process worked and the men in the arena had all the support and intelligence they needed to accomplish the mission.

Overseas, simple coordination for latrine facilities for over 25 personnel can be a major problem. Sanitary conditions need to be maintained to ensure the force remains well and healthy to accomplish the mission. A force that gets sick from some parasite will put them out of action as rapidly as an enemy bullet. For extended operations, sleeping arrangements need to be worked out to house the force and allow them proper rest and not expose them to the constant commotion that comes from a TOC. This may be solved by a simple issue of eye patches and ear plugs.

## EMPOWER YOUR LEADERSHIP

Empowerment is critical to ensure mission success. Your subunit leaders must have responsibility and understand that it is up to them to make it happen. This includes using their tactical thoughts and input and ensuring they are always part of the planning process. This "empowerment" accomplishes several things. First, it requires each subunit leader to take initiative and have their personal system squared away and ready for the fight. While these subunit leaders are planning, usually their troops have the time to tailor their equipment for the fight. The planning leader will have little time to do this because of the planning requirement. If they have a cohesive team, the team will usually take care of it for them.

Empowerment also puts the mental and physical responsibility of the team on the team leader's mind. This creates an added positive pressure to exceed standards when one knows that other lives are at risk. They subtly know that their skill at planning is critical to ensure the survival of the team and successful mission accomplishment. Leaders at this level should ensure they are always mentally and physically ready for the challenge and that their teams are up for it. To ensure that your team is ready to conduct rehearsals, rapid and accurate information must be pushed down to them in a timely manner. This can be accomplished in two ways. First, the team leaders each go directly to their prospective teams and relay the information. If planning is going on, one team leader can go and inform a member of each team. A second technique is to have one Assistant Team Leader (ATL) report to the planning area, brief them and have them deliver the information to the rest of the teams. The information pushed down to the ATL could be as simple as an additional equipment requirement for the mission or something critical as information on the number of bad guys and hostages.

Further, team leaders who plan together will be more apt to work with other team leaders regarding the critical portions of the mission such as alternate breach points and link-up points inside or outside of the target. Alternate breach points are always planned and should a team not be able to get into their primary breach point, the team leader will direct them to the alternate. When moving to an alternate breach point, a team will be pushing through and into another team's area, coming in behind them to link-up, either moving through the team to their front, or pushing them ahead further into their area of responsibility.

Link-up points are another critical area that team leaders need to plan and rehearse. A Link-up point is a physical location inside the target where two friendly forces will find themselves pointing guns at each other. Sometimes a bad guy runs from one team area and runs into another team and the gun fight starts. Teams need to know when to push and when to hold and when to push through should you wait on a link-up team too long. In past incidences, link-up teams have mistakenly fired on each other, mistaking a member of their sister element of being a threat.

# THE QUICKEST AND MOST EFFICIENT WAY TO PLAN

### Alert the Force

Ensure that the system you use to alert and gather the force works and is simple and effective. Have a primary and secondary method of communication available.

### Report

All members should report in and leaders should be given a brief mission statement that can be passed to all team members. If an assistant team leader gets in first, he can pass the info the team leader upon their arrival. If the TL is late, the ATL should begin the planning process.

### Begin Planning

After briefing their teams, the team leader should report to a central planning area to receive an information update and command guidance. Other key things happen at this time, but this being an open source of information, I will not elaborate on special team tactics and deployments.

### Pass info/prepare rehearsal areas

As information becomes available, it should be pushed down to the end users (teams) as rapidly as possible so they can tailor their gear for the mission. Also, certain teams may be responsible for getting together a rehearsal site and this can be as elaborate as doing a live fire scenario in a local shooting house or as simple as a walk through tape drill on the ground.

### Brief the Plan

Once the plan is formulated and the commander gives the go ahead, available assets should be assembled and briefed as a group, if at all possible. This technique involves everyone looking at the plan, not to sharp shoot it, but to look at common danger and problem areas that need to be addressed. So when you talk about link-ups you understand which team you are going to see.

### Rehearse

Rehearsals should be conducted from the bottom level up and then the actions on the objective first. Hopefully, once assistant team leaders got the word of the mission and got their gear ready, they should have taken their individual teams and started to do walk through rehearsals on their own. They can walk through and discuss exterior movement, breach point procedures, interior movement, CQB procedures and consolidation procedures for the target. They can also review medical procedures and do an equipment shakedown to ensure all the mission essential gear is present and functioning. Much of this concerns individual and team actions.

### Fix problems

Rehearsals should start with all teams working on how they are going to take down the target, or actions on the objective. They should do this several times to get it done right and then the rehearsal staff should throw in some problems to make the force think and ensure their back up plans work and are viable. Also, rehearsals will point out any glaring problems with the plan. Once this is accomplished, you can then work on your movement phase and putting the entire package together.

### Re-Rehearse, Re-Brief and integrate all assets into the plan

If there are too may problems with the initial plan, leadership should re-brief the entire plan to the group. Too many changes will confuse everyone to include key leaders as to what the current plan is. At the individual level, men need to have a simple and streamlined thought process as to what is going to happen on the mission and their role in it. Taking the time to rebrief will save everyone a world of headaches.

### Prepare for mission execution

Once final rehearsals are complete, the force can catch their breath and standby for the execution phase. It may come soon or the action may take days. Leaders should act accordingly and ensure that the men are not burned out by leaning on the edge too long and too hard. Take down time (rest) as appropriate and ensure the men are rotated if it looks like they are becoming fatigued or burned-out. Then re-rehearse actions as needed to keep the force sharp.

### In Conclusion

Leadership planning is a critical component of an operation and must be rehearsed and refined as any other action. Further, junior leadership should be continually exposed to this process to cultivate future leaders and shorten their learning curve as it relates to their leadership growth. Leadership training will be covered in the next chapter.

## KEY POINTS

- DEVELOP A SIMPLE AND EFFECTIVE PLANNING SYSTEM AND THEN REHEARSE IT
- EMPOWER AND USE ALL AVAILABLE SUB-UNIT LEADERS AND THEIR TALENT TO DEVELOP A PLAN
- REHEARSE THE PLAN AND IF THERE ARE TOO MANY CHANGES, RE-BRIEF THE ENTIRE PLAN

# CHAPTER TEN

# TEACHING LEADERSHIP

*"I will not stand by and watch this great country destroy itself under mediocre leadership that drifts from one crisis to the next, eroding our national will and purpose. We have come together here because the American people deserve better from those to who they entrust our nation's highest offices, and we stand united in our resolve to do something about it."*

Ronald Reagan

- THE CURRENT SYSTEM
- LEADERSHIP SHOULD BE A REQUIRED CLASS
- WORKING LEADERSHIP OR MANAGEMENT LEADERSHIP
- TRAIN EFFICIENTLY AND REALISTICALLY
- FOCUS ON WHAT IS IMPORTANT, SAFETY, TECHNICAL AND TACTICAL
- THE HARD CASES
- KEY POINTS

## THE "Q" COURSE

I was fortunate to serve under a man in the late 1990's who I thought was a great leader. When he was in his mid-40's, he went through the Special Forces Qualification course as a student. The extraordinary point about this was that he was a full Bird Colonel who was taking over command of the entire Special Forces Training

Division and had already completed the training. When asked, "Why are you going through as a private? His answer was simple. "If I don't know what is broke, I can't fix it."

I remember this same officer as our section commander, always leading by example. One day we had a back-to-back "Gut Check" that consisted of multiple events. We started with a multi-event round robin in the gym and then moved outside for more physical tests. It was hot outside, 105-110 degrees and we grabbed our rucksacks and did an eight-mile road march. It was so hot, that MP's stopped and asked us if we had permission to march in the heat. We ignored them and kept on trucking. The march ended at the obstacle course where we went through the 26 obstacles and then moved back to the main building. There we reported to the pool and swam 500 meters non-stop to finish out the morning. This mini-gut check was to be one of many that I fondly recall. Geared toward the individual, no one yelled or screamed at you. You could move at whatever pace you deemed appropriate and which would give you enough energy to complete the next phase. You always had to be smart about this. If you put too much energy into one event, you might fail on the next one or one more down the line. You never knew how many more events were to come and this helped strengthen your mind for the unknown and it prepared you to deal with the unexpected. You learned to move at about 80 percent speed, always keeping a bit in reserve. Being tired actually helped your wandering mind by taking away all the excess energy that causes you to lose focus. It also helps you to take one step at a time and focus on the next step.

## AFTER ACTION COMMENTS

### Sustain:

- Don't be afraid to get your hands dirty

### Improve:

- Cultivate and promote more leaders as described above

# THE CURRENT SYSTEM

In my opinion, the current military system of leadership takes two very different paths. First, is the enlisted path operating under the theory that you must be tactically proficient in your job before you can move into a leadership position. The other route is that of the officer corps which supports the thought process that you only need to be familiar with the job and you can be a successful leader. Both courses achieve their desired results, but I would argue that the latter breeds mediocrity and could be much more efficient. This efficiency equates to saving more of our soldiers lives on the battlefield.

The enlisted route to leadership begins with the building blocks of the unit, the fire team. For example, a soldier enters the Army and begins a career as a private. He learns all the soldier skills and soon will migrate across the different jobs of the squad. This course begins with a three-month basic training and then continues into a four to six week Advanced Individual Training (AIT) in their specialty area. This specialty area might be infantry, mechanical or an administrative position. The infantry soldier moves from their AIT training unit to a rifleman position in either a mechanized or light infantry unit. Once they master this skill, they may be a machine gunner, or they may move to an anti-tank weapon or to a grenade launcher. As they move from job to job, they get a great deal more experience and intimacy with their weapon systems allowing them to understand their individual capabilities and limitations. They also become an integral part of a fire team allowing them to understand the capabilities and limitations of that unit. They live the job day to day and become a professional at their trade. With the passage of time, schooling and testing, the team members are then selected into the ranks of the Non-Commissioned Officer (NCO) Corps. They will begin their NCO career and management of a four to five person fire team. Their next progression in rank is the Squad Leader who controls two fire teams. Beyond the Squad Leader rank, they may become a Platoon Sergeant who controls three to four Squads consisting of two fire teams each. The rank of Platoon Sergeant is generally the highest tactical rank that can be attained as an NCO in the regular Army. Beyond the platoon sergeant rank is the First Sergeant whose job is an administrative position which supports the company commander. First Sergeants are in charge of the "beans and bullets." In effect, once an enlisted man reaches the pinnacle of his tactical career, he is moved to a logistical position within the fighting element. A good commanding officer will heed the advice of their First Sergeant and try and drain every bit of tactical knowledge out of them. Some do, some don't

The officer route to career progression is a bit different. About 70 percent of the U.S. Army officers come from the Reserve Officer Training Corps or ROTC. Their general course migration begins as a college student who is "recruited" into the program. Last count, there were 270 plus ROTC programs at our nation's campus's across the United States. These programs are under the supervision of the host university. These programs are generally a four-year program that takes a college student from Military Science I level (MS-I) to MS-IV during this time. Typically the student takes one college accredited Military Science course per semester with one lab a week. Students are taught basic soldier skills at a more informal level on campus. They are organized in a Battalion, which is comprised of two companies consisting of three to four platoons and squads. The average school has 60-100 ROTC cadets in the program at one time. MS I and II years are the fun years or "hook" as I liked to refer to it, where the cadre is nice to the students and encourages them to "contract" with the program in order to become Second Lieutenants in the Army. The third and fourth year MS III and MS IV have two different goals. The goal in the MS III year is to get the students ready for a five-week summer camp held at Ft. Lewis, Washington. This Summer camp has gone from a graded event to a pass/fail event to ensure that the Army gets their required numbers. Once a student passes camp, they return to campus and then begin their MS-IV year where they begin "transition to officer ship" and prepare to become commissioned second lieutenants in the Army. The MS IV year is generally taught by the Professor of Military Science (PMS), who most frequently holds the rank of Lieutenant Colonel (LTC). Once they complete this year, they go on to become commissioned officers, that is, if they graduate college. Many of these cadets are not academically aligned and must first graduate college to receive their commissions. I have witnessed cadets who took two plus years past projected dates to get commissioned because their grades were so poor. PMS's are reluctant to dis-enroll these students because their own success is judged/evaluated on how many cadets they commission. It is a never ending battle.

Once a cadet is commissioned, they are sent to an Officer Basic Course (OBC) that can range from four to six months. ROTC allows cadets to "slide" through their program in the belief that it is OBC's job to weed them out. Unfortunately, the OBC is under the same pressure as the PMS to pass as many second lieutenants into the Army as possible. Their feelings are probably much the same; let the operational units weed out these new lieutenants. It is a vicious cycle where no one puts their foot down and culls the herd. Consequently, the Army now has a sub-standard leader that has slid through the process and is now in charge of 30-40 soldiers who are headed for combat. Scary.

The problem lies with the fact that the Army puts the newest and least experienced leader in charge of the large tactical maneuver group of people and then deploys them into a potentially high-risk situation where lives are at stake. This system will work in a peacetime administrative environment where no one generally dies. Instead the system should be geared toward a worst case war-time footing where lives hang in the balance. There are several solutions to this problem, but the entrenched leadership system that our services promote will not be changed without a catastrophic failure.

Further problems with the officer system lie with the cut-throat evaluation system where only "one" can get the top evaluation and all fight for it. This competition produces more negative results than positive. It draws the dark side of human nature promoting mistrust and a non-cooperative working environment. Officers are now competing for the golden egg and their shot at promotion with little concern for their men. Generally, every commander with something to prove or gain, takes command and drives the company into the ground for his two years of service and then moves on to his next position. I have witnessed this more than once.

## LEADERSHIP SHOULD BE A REQUIRED CLASS

We should begin in our elementary schools to develop leaders and seeking out more at each grade level, bringing a few more into the fold with each passing year. This thought process would greatly help our society and we would not be stuck choosing a president to lead our nation who is the "lesser of two evils." Some leaders will naturally emerge through the process. Many will emerge after the proper catalyst. Currently, some service personnel are fortunate to serve under good leaders for an extended period of time and then are forced to serve under a bad one. Hopefully, they have to endure the stupidity and ignorance that affects their work and life for a short time. Soon these victims become disgusted and think to themselves, I can do his job, and be much better. In effect, this discomfort is a motivation for leadership.

Are instructors leaders? You bet. They take control of a group for a determined period of time and move them from one goal to another and their influence and style can have a great impact on the momentum and strides that the class has. I have found as an instructor that when you are assigned to teach a subject and you take the time to properly prepare, you will learn a great deal more than the average instructor who is simply out to punch a ticket. For example, when I teach instructor courses in the law enforcement community, I require students to prepare and deliver a block of instruction to a class of new students and to sit through all the blocks of instruction. For example, in a rifle instructor class which is four days in length, I assign blocks of instruction to instructor students on the first day so as they might take the time to study, learn, prepare and rehearse their block of instruction prior to the end of the course. The day following the final day of the course, I run a basic class of tactical rifle to new students. The instructors are the ones delivering all blocks of instruction to the new students under my supervision. These new instructors are required to attend all the new student blocks of instruction at which time they see the material again and it is reinforced one more time.

This technique does several things. First, it allows the instructor students to see the material several times and the class twice. The students see the material during the instructor class again when they study at night, and again during the student class when either they deliver the block or listen to another instructor who gives the block of instruction. Repetition is the key to grasping and understanding the material. I generally find that if an instructor puts out a great deal of information, the student generally only retains 50-70 percent if they are lucky and if they take notes. I see a great deal of students that don't take notes and probably only get up to 50 percent of the information if they are lucky.

Using this technique, I believe that leadership should be a required class and that students should be required at times to study it, regurgitate to an audience, and then put it into practical application. Leaders have the ability to impact work and life issues and to have a positive influence on both. Leaders in a civilian community can greatly improve productivity by simply using and transferring leadership techniques illustrated in this book. The same goes for the impact they have on the lives that they touch and influence in a day-to-day work and leadership role. They have the ability to make the workplace a fun and enjoyable experience or a daily dull grind.

Where can we apply these classes? Our military already uses them, but typically this approach is not used in our schools and colleges. Some will argue that these methods are used. They may, but not in an efficient, organized and structured way. I see too many instructors that have never led, teaching leadership classes and seminars. Do what I say and not what I do has become the standard answer in education and in government. This is not leading by example.

## TRAIN EFFICIENTLY AND REALISTICALLY

As a leader, you should use the same leadership style and system in the administrative world as you would use in training or combat. Nothing should change from training to combat or administration to business. The staff that is designated to support you should have the ability to ensure that training and training exercises are setup and run at a very high level. Exercises should be routinely run to ensure that command elements are versed in the proper solutions for the tactical problems they will face. In the military, simple range fire exercises or complex targets will be used by good leaders and they will use the available assets to ensure soldiers get the most out of every exercise. Civilian leaders can easily do the same in their corporate training.

In the law enforcement community, tactical teams are always looking for buildings to train with. Generally a building that is going to be destroyed works best because no one has to worry about clean up or accidentally breaking anything. It can be a training distracter to spend more time cleaning up a target than you did actually training on one. Leaders should always have someone in their command staff on the lookout for buildings that are getting ready to be torn down. These are diamonds in the rough and breaching techniques can be practiced to break doors and windows. These are especially good if they are used as a "surprise" target, where the tactical team members have never been inside and it is a unknown floor plan. This gives them the most realistic training situation that will set them up for success on a real world target.

## WORKING LEADERSHIP OR MANAGEMENT LEADERSHIP

The choice is yours when you accept promotion to a leadership position. You can accept the status quo or you can take care of your people and excel.   As I have mentioned before, dynamic and progressive leadership requires more energy then those being led. Many who accept the leadership role feel that they have "earned" their right to take a break. Nothing could be further from the truth. True leaders don't punch time clocks. They come as early as needed and stay as late as needed to get the job accomplished.

When a leader takes over a new position they will generally spend quite a bit of time setting up their "personal system" of leadership and doing business. This could be reviewing the current practices, developing their own administrative system that allows them to efficiently deal with the paperwork requirements of the job, or just performing the daily day-to-day operations required of the new position.  When I moved to a new position of leadership, I found that the days were filled with meetings, counseling subordinates, and solving problems of the day. This left little time to get the paperwork accomplished.  I found that coming in early a few days a week allowed me to get ahead on all the paperwork.  This approach enabled me to keep my time open during the day to "keep the machine running."  This early-to-work concept also allowed me to get more work accomplished faster with a total focus towards the job and without the distractions of the daily business, phones and individuals wanting to talk or shoot the breeze.  It also allowed me to focus on the daily business with little or no pressure.

Did I get paid for my extra time? No, but it did provide me with a bit of sanity and a stress reduction. It also gave me the chance to keep a physical training program that helped reduce my stress. Why did I do it without pay? It was the right thing to do to ensure all the leadership functions continued in a seamless manner and that I could take care of my people in the proper manner without a disruption to their system. Too many times Americans want to get paid for every time they fart. That's BS.

The wrong type of leader is the "manager." These are typically the people who punch the clock for every second they work. They watch it closer than their employees do. They also inconvenience their employees by disrupting their schedules to accommodate their own, so they can be more comfortable in their workday. "Self-Service versus Selfless-Service." This is the simplest way I can describe the difference between the manager and the leader.

## FOCUS ON WHAT IS IMPORTANT, SAFETY, TECHNICAL AND TACTICAL

Leaders need to understand the technical, tactical and safety aspects of the job, so they make more informed and intelligent decisions on a course of action. If a certain course of action seems risky then the leader must have the knowledge base to approve, disapprove or help modify the plan for successful implementation.

Safety is also an important factor in this equation. Even in combat safety measures need to be adhered to. Friendly fire or "fratricide" can induce as many casualties as enemy fire. It happens in every conflict and it takes proper planning and identification to ensure that friendly troops don't fire on each other in the heat of battle. During the invasion of Panama, we almost lost more soldiers from friendly fire than from enemy fire. Individuals may argue this point, but I have witnessed several friendly fire incidents first hand that were covered up and reported as hostile fire to save face for the unit as well as the individual who pulled the trigger. As the lethality of our weapons systems grow, so must our training.

Next, as a leader you must understand the technical aspects of the plan and what assets it takes to accomplish the desired mission. This ranges from logistical assets such as trucks, fuel, etc., to helicopters and planes. Besides movement, you might need an ammo re-supply should a prolonged contact take place. You will also need trained people to deliver the ammo. Should you be staying more than 72 hours, you will probably need food and water. Also, should someone become hurt or killed, you need to have a medical support plan in place to provide extraction of your casualties.

Finally, if you do not understand the tactical aspects of a situation, your men could miss an important detail in the planning phase and become trapped or expose themselves to more danger than necessary. Requiring several people to review your plan will act as a safety valve of sorts. You should have several other team leaders with tactical experience that are looking not only at their portion of the plan, but also the bigger picture.

## THE HARD CASES

Occasionally, the civilian world has a "hard case" to deal with. I define a hard case as one of those unpleasant incidents where someone is hurt or killed as a result of training, daily work, or a mission. The law enforcement and military arena provide the easiest examples to point out. For example, a person can be injured or killed as a result of friendly fire during a real world mission or training exercise. Generally the consequence of such an incident is that all training is ceased, interviews begin and statements are taken. At the incident level, where a specific team is involved, usually one of two type teams are present. One is the team who has been together for a long time through thick and thin. This team sticks together on their story and generally point outs what happened and who is at fault. If they are a professional team, the team member who screwed up and demonstrated the poor judgment will stand up and admit fault by describing how he shot when he should have held his fire. Much depends on the atmosphere that leaders of the group have built over time. If leaders always preach and demonstrate honesty, integrity and candor, then the men will step forward without hesitation. Occasionally, the professional team will try and protect the individual by altering the story a bit by leaving out a detail here or there. This can cause problems when future problems arise and they will continue their pattern of cover-up.

The other team that can be involved in the incident is the team that has been newly formed or has self-serving leadership. Depending on the professionalism of the leadership and the guts of the team leader, the team may or may not bring the proper information to light. The new TL can be pressured by team members and help the "good guy" who was involved. The incident may be covered up. Once in a while, a TL will stand up as a leader, call a spade a spade and set a new standard for the team. This may be difficult to do, but it is the right answer. This is a critical call for leaders in Special Operation teams and units. A good leader can turn a negative experience into a positive learning and building experience.

Too often I have witnessed the team spending more time covering up incidents rather than fixing them. It is far easier to analyze the incident in a professional and unbiased way, rather than to cover it up and have the same or another team make a similar mistake down the road. The true leader will put emotions and heartache aside once the facts are in. The true leader will recreate the training accident for everyone to examine and show alternate ways of fixing the problem. This process will ensure adequate safety measures are put in place to keep it from happening again. This process will be painful, especially if there is the loss of a long time friend and team member. But it begins the healing process much faster if everyone takes a hard look at what happened, figures out where the true fault lies and implements a solution to fixing it.

Weak leaders that lack the intestinal fortitude will run for cover from negative publicity or the potential political career impact of accidents. Such leaders aide in the cover up of an incident where it would be better served to inform the entire group of what happened to prevent it again in the future. Approaching problems in this manner is akin to putting a bandage over an infected wound. This will cause the wound to fester and kill more good tissue. Instead, this situation requires that you clean out the wound thoroughly and quickly before bandaging it. Otherwise you will be doing double work and treating for an infection that will require more attention and prevents the patient from not returning to work for a longer time. The same philosophy applies to a critical incident. You need to bring out all the facts as quickly as possible and address all the concerns of the men. Usually, this effectively puts the issue to bed, stopping all rumors, blame and stories that can create morale problems. Failure to quickly address the situation will allow for excuses and similar events to occur. This situation now requires twice the work for a leader to fix future issues and it also damages the leader's credibility. True leadership will get to the facts, talk it out, recreate it, implement change, and move on.

## KEY POINTS

As a leader, surround yourself with competent and aggressive subunit leaders and then empower them to do your job. You will soon be surprised how easy your job becomes. I have watched weak leaders surround themselves with weak subordinates and or individuals, some who owe them their allegiance because the leader pulled them out of a self-induced crisis. This type of leader generally self implodes somewhere down the line as their subunit leaders are weak and are doomed to repeat the same mistakes in the future.

Negative attitudes are the hardest flaw to fix when you accept a new leadership position. Come in quiet, on your team's level; work, listen, and implement change as needed. Give your team credit for the change. This praise and proactive attitude goes a long way. Do not reward failure or lack of effort. If you don't have a good leader, tell them face-to-face. If they cannot or choose not to improve, get rid of them and let them know why. This is the most honorable thing you can do for them. The alternative is to pass them to another position of responsibility where they can negatively affect more people. Also, choosing lap dogs as sub leaders will only cause you further legal and morale problems.

"Selection is a never ending process," and it applies to you too. If you can't overcome mental shortcomings or lack of motivation, move over and make room for someone who can. This also goes for being burned out. I have a great deal of respect for someone who is burned out, knows it, and removes themselves from a leadership position where they can infect a team with their poor or tired attitude. This also applies to leaders who have overwhelming health or family problems.

Finally, avoid setting up a "dream team," that you rely on instead of improving the entire force to rise to the challenge.  For example, some leaders rely on a chosen few who do 80 percent of missions or work.  Poor leaders are either too insecure or lazy to work to bring the entire force to the same high level of competence.  I have observed commanders rely on a dream team to do business.  In one such incident, a Swat team's "select" members were out of town competing in a national competition.  The rest of the force had to perform a real world mission and fell short.  This caused a serious self-inflicted injury that resulted in five team members being reassigned.  These are problems that could have been avoided by ensuring all team members were trained to the same standard. True leaders put politics and the political games aside because the greatest honor of a leader is to take care of their soldiers or subordinates.

## KEY POINTS

- Make The Hard Right Choices As Leader.
- Put More Effort In Than Less.
- Surround Yourself With Strong, Effective Leaders.

# CHAPTER ELEVEN

# COUNSELING
# AND MENTORSHIP

*"A neglected skill"*

- NATURE OF THE BEAST
- COUNSELING
- THE IMPORTANCE OF THE OUTSIDE PERSPECTIVE
- ADMINISTRATIVE REQUIREMENTS
- TOTALITY OF AN INCIDENT
- TECHNIQUES AND COURSES OF ACTION

## "REMEMBER YOUR FRONT SIGHT"

"Remember your front sight" was probably the most memorable and lasting statement a leader has ever said to me before going in to combat. It came from our group sergeant major the night we were going to execute combat operations in a country that was finishing its downward spiral. He stated, "Tomorrow night you will be in combat." A few days earlier this country had crossed a line of no return and security forces had killed an American officer. The U.S. military and political leadership finally had the reason they needed to conduct a large scale military operation and remove the country's corrupt government, one that we probably had some help in establishing.

We loaded our gear and flew into country. We retrieved our cots and set them up as we had done a couple of times before. We then waited. At the "gumby" level, I carried the M203 grenade launcher and a few extra rounds. The tropical heat was playing hell on our bodies and acclimating was a bitch. The heat caused our bodies to pour water out. Members of another group tried to wear their heavy Kevlar vests and conduct training, but the heat set them straight. I watched as more than one man came back from a training exercise and collapsed on the hanger floor from heat exhaustion. Soon they would be hooked up to a 1000 ml I.V. bag and once it was gone they would probably get one more. The rule of thumb I learned during medical classes was that when you had to piss, your body was starting to get enough fluid back.

We found that you could not physically put enough water back into your body to make up for the loss caused by the body armor we wore at the time. The armor coupled with the constant heat would put you out of action as quickly as an enemy's bullet. The leadership had a real dilemma to deal with in this situation. We were tasked to perform multiple operations, either day or night, and this tasking said nothing about I.V.'s being plugged into us while we were conducting these missions. The "risk vs. gamble" option was put out and the decision was made not to wear our Kevlar vests. Instead, we would generally wear a pistol belt and chest pack or LCE/LBE (load carrying equipment/load bearing equipment vest) of our choosing. In the end, the individual had to be able to hump their load mission after mission and be ready to perform for the next one. I was shocked that the chain of command had let us make that decision; but I was also impressed. The group commander was a no-nonsense guy who was not afraid of making smart decisions or let subordinate leaders make wise decisions. He did not look at his career first as so many did at that time.

The combat operations or live fire ARTEP as I referred to it, (Army Training Exercise) was kicked off on schedule and our sister element led in on the initial wave. They were successful in their hit and returned with minor casualties. The overall commander, a consummate ticket-puncher allowed us out the next day to go to work. We were able to flush the elusive target after a week of beating the bush. We conducted over 40 hits in a week , keeping the bad guy moving and guessing. While conventional units were trying to push through the city on a dedicated time line, we were able to roam free from one side of the city to the other. As intel came in, we hit targets in all areas, keeping the momentum and presence of U.S. forces intact. We would jump on a neighborhood and rumble in, shaking the ground with our approach and jump on a target of our choosing, reeking havoc for a short time until we were sure that our desired person was not there. We would then move on to other areas of interest.

Generally, no one opposed us on our missions. On one instance, two guys committed suicide by shooting at us as we neared our target building. The vehicles in which we were riding opened up with at least four Browning M-2 .50 caliber machine guns at what I still remember was the most beautiful cones of fire I had ever seen. The tracers could be seen in the night, flowing from all the guns into one spot and upon impact, became unstable and erratic. To add to their firepower, we poured out of the vehicles like ants, launching a few tracer rounds or 40mm high explosive grenade at the beaten zone. The two individuals, who were probably a local home defense force, made the deadly mistake of firing at our 12 plus vehicles. They did this with an Uzi submachine gun. Dumb. We were hunters on a mission and ready to do business. Their world quickly came to an end.

We had been running hard for three or four days and we ran into these two jokers on a night operation. We had executed numerous raids to this point and we were getting burned out, mentally and physically. When the lead bad guy opened fire, we pushed out from the vehicles in all directions and set-up a loose perimeter. Our team went straight ahead and made a right turn and then pushed a little deeper down the street. We did not know where the target building was, but we were going to push our perimeter out far enough to protect the force. We made contact with some locals who were the "home guard" of the next street/neighborhood 30 yards to our front at the next intersection. We jacked them up and put them on the ground. Searching them, we found a .38 revolver on one. I stuffed into a cargo pocket on my pants. We flex tied the man who had the gun and dumped him into a flower bed across the street where Tony and I pulled security down the intersecting street. Gary and Al stayed on the main street to our front. All of a sudden, someone poked out of a darkened house and pumped six rounds down the street in front of us. No one returned fire. It sounded like someone with a revolver shot their wad and tucked back in their house playing it safe. During this time, Tony and I saw folks moving around on top of the hill above the target building and vehicles. I held my fire as I did not see any gun, but suddenly a .50 cal from the vehicles sent a burst up and I could follow the tracers to their target. I swagged it (best guess) and sent one 40 mm from my M203 grenade launcher up into the area the tracers had just impacted. If nothing else, I hoped to help keep them honest and their heads down. We never did take any fire from that area. While covering Tony's six-o'clock, the guy who we had laid in the flower bed called to us and asked if could move. We laughed and told him "No." The truth was that we had forgotten all about him.

We got the word to pull back and things got hairy. We did not know where our other security positions were, so we bounded back using cover until we linked up our guys. They were switched on and recognized our movements, shapes and outlines and held their fire. A few of the guys were holding on the other side of a vehicle that had been parked sideways in the street to prevent other vehicles from entering the neighborhood. You could see vehicles all up and down the street set up in the same fashion. Before we moved to the opposite side of the car, I glanced down and saw someone lying in the street on the other side of the car from our guys. Apparently when the shooting started, they hit the ground and were too scared to make a noise. They stayed there the entire time. I told the team what they had and they talked to him and told him it was okay to go back home. It seemed like we had only been on this target for an hour or two, searching buildings, consolidating dead and wounded.

We pulled security by the vehicles and waited for the word to mount up. We were smoked, physically tired and running on empty. I equate a firefight to that of a parachute jump, but worse in terms of energy expended. Usually I tell folks that one parachute jump robs your body of about eight hours worth of "juice" or energy. The same goes for a fire fight or engagement. We had been running for three or four days straight doing hits in the daytime heat and it was catching up with us. Prior to and during a hit, you would get an adrenaline dump that would keep you pumped up for an hour or so, but then you wanted to crash. Pulling security in a buddy team, you would tell you buddy to rack out for a few minutes while you would pull security and then you would take your turn. You had to get rest whenever you could. We received the word to mount up, collected our team, and remounted our vehicle.

We started our movement back toward the center of the city where we ran into a conventional force that was on foot. We got the word that some of their privates were trying to put their anti-tank weapons into action and engage us. This is one of the things that unnerved me about combat. These folks had been getting sniped at and were understandably edgy. Even though we were traveling in U.S. vehicles, of which the bad guys had none, our soldiers still got scared and wanted to pull the trigger on this "perceived" threat. Looking ragged with a three-day growth of beard, we were developing that hard look of a "don't fuck with me" appearance. A fire support captain attached to that unit came out of a dark doorway and looked at us and a couple of our vehicles and asked "who are you guys." Norm sounded off with "we're the ghost busters." I laughed to myself and told the captain to talk with the officer on our lead vehicle. He kept looking at us saying, "Nobody will give us any fire support." Spectre will not even drop illumination for us. I did not doubt why. No telling who this unit would fire up in their travels.

We got the word to hold fast and two of the trail vehicles took off in the direction of our last target. Come to find out it was good that we stopped. During the stop, one of the guys on the rear tracks was looking at the back of a helmet of who he thought was his battle buddy named Kit. When they stopped and his buddy turned around it was the wrong guy. Evidently, during the lull in the last action, it was Kit's turn to nap and he did. But when his battle buddy remounted vehicles, he took the back of the helmet of another guy for Kit and did not see his face. Kit was still asleep on the ground at the raid site. Evidently, Kit woke up shortly after our departure, looking around and nobody was there. He thought "What the fuck?!" and got into some bushes. He then got his radio out and started to make calls. At about the same time, our guys realized that Kit was not in the vehicle. Kit got on the air and let them know his situation. The two trail vehicles went back and recovered him without incident.

## AFTER ACTION POINTS

### Sustain:

- Maintain vigilance around friendly troops.

### Improve:

- Get face to face accountability whenever possible.
- Ensure your battle buddy is accounted for.

## NATURE OF THE BEAST

The "Nature of the Beast" term could also be used to describe the "nature of humans." While not all humans fall into the same category, a majority are affected by the same human conditions, good or bad that can weaken our individual character. These conditions will in turn affect our drive or spirit. As a group, we humans try and meet society standards. Notice, I said meet. The level or "bar" is set by society and their feeling or "attitude" at the time. If society is in a kinder-gentler mood, the bar may be set lower to accommodate human weakness and not hurt any feelings. This bar can be applied to everything in our society from crime and punishment, to social tolerances and perceptions to external problems outside our country.

When in the kinder-gentler mood, society becomes more tolerant of failure. It is accepted and the blame is diverted from the individual or group to society or someone or something that has no feelings. Such is the case for the 9/11 failures. No government agency wants to call a spade a spade and say "These people or this person screwed up." We as a society have become accustomed to excuses and readily accept them even if they fail to correct the problems that may arise in the future. Ultimately, no one is held accountable and the problematic behavior continues. This attitude is just part of the system. I believe that we can control our own destiny and behavior. Contrary to what is taught in schools, there are good students and there are bad students just as there are good people and bad people in this world. We need to understand that we have mechanisms at our disposal to correct bad behavior. I refer to such mechanisms as "counseling."

## COUNSELING

Counseling is the process we use to correct behavior that does not fit into the desired scheme of things. Through counseling we advise or give suggestions to encourage positive behavior. I would say that this definition is darn close to that of leadership except that counseling occurs at the individual level. Counseling can go up or down, left or right. More commonly it goes down to subordinates, but you can counsel peers in an informal way. This also applies to your boss, though it would probably behoove you to ensure your delivery method of counseling is respectful and professional.

The counseling of peers should at a minimum, consist of three forms. Those being **initial, quarterly and exit counseling**. Initial counseling should consist of both a "get to know" counseling and an orientation/information counseling. The get to know counseling is just that, getting to know your new person at the individual level, taking a personal interest in them, their personal history or life, their family and their future goals. This counseling should break down any preconceived barriers or walls established by the mystique of the organization. For example, an officer that is selected for a position to a new tactical team probably has a great deal of preconceived ideas as to the organization, mission or structure of the team or unit. This would be a great time to dispel these myths and set the story straight. Another suggestion is to do this with your next in charge subordinate or at least during an introduction. Once the individual session is complete, you probably want to schedule a follow up session for more of an orientation to the new organization.

A simple suggestion for a follow up orientation is to give the new person a binder containing all the organizations rules and SOP's to look at and review for a week or so. Schedule the next orientation session so that the new person has time to read and ask questions about the rules and SOP's. At the next session go over any highlights that you see as reoccurring problem areas and then have the new member sign a memorandum of understanding as to having read the book. This will help dispel any future excuses such as "I didn't know" or "I wasn't told." It might even be wise to assign the new member a sponsor who will work closely with them for the next few weeks or months to get their feet on the ground. This new member "battle buddy" concept generally ensures that a team concept is present and it will greatly strengthen the individual's new view of the organization and the team oriented work ethic.

Once the individual has their feet on the ground, the unit leader should conduct quarterly or semi-annual one-on-one counseling. This approach clears the air of any developing misconceptions and ensures that everyone is working toward a common goal. Occasionally, individuals have a perception of themselves that is not shared by leadership. You owe it to this person to let them know. Individuals may be totally unaware of what they are doing, not doing or their current level of performance. It is the leader's job to look such individuals in the eye and let them know. This should be done in a tactful manner and the more professional and sincere the individual, the smaller the hammer you will need. Even well meaning good people are sometimes dumber than a box of rocks and require a much bigger hammer to get the points through to them. Some personalities are so self confident and overbearing that you have to chop them down a notch just to get one or two points across. Evaluate your target and then choose your delivery method.

One method to break the ice during counseling sessions is to let the person talk first and burn up their nervous energy, then you can ease into your counseling. Sometimes your counseling may consist of nothing more than saying you're doing a great job and keep it up. Either way, give the person a chance to get comfortable and establish the session as a positive one and not a one-sided ass chewing. When bringing out deficiencies, have your facts and figures straight and offer suggestions on how to improve. Ask them what they intend to do to improve their weaknesses. By allowing them to feed you back information, you are ensuring that they understand and comprehend what you said.

Exit counseling was used to help make the team or organization stronger. I generally do this once an employee is designated to leave an organization. Once all evaluations are complete, I want to ensure the individual understands that nothing will be held against them once they depart, nor will any evaluations be changed. Generally this will produce an honest and informative session that can be used to better the organization. No matter the candor and honesty that is established in individual counseling sessions, occasionally individuals are apprehensive about bringing out negative points about internal team issues feeling that it is a team problem to work out. This technique will sometimes bring to light issues that you are unaware of and will keep you abreast of problems that might fester.

**Spot reports, achievement awards or "pulse checks"** are other types of counseling that can take a formal or informal status. Spot reports or "blue cards" were cards used in ROTC to denote a one time good or bad incident involving a cadet. These spot reports were generally issued for negative conduct, but could as easily be issued for positive conduct. Too many times in life we are only worried about bringing out the problems in a person rather than the good points. Good spot reports add ammunition and substance to counseling and yearly evaluations and reinforce positive behavior. Taking about five minutes to write, you can check the block, jot down notes of the incident, and talk to the person about it in a formal or informal setting. If it is a good incident you can praise them at the individual level in front of their team or the group. Keeping the positive record and others like it will allow you to articulate it later on counseling reports and yearly evaluations as well as to pinpoint and substantiate higher performance levels given. Too many times we scramble for input at the last possible moment to substantiate an evaluation. In some cases, evaluations were downgraded because leaders did not do a good job of counseling or record keeping. The individual in question suffers because of this.

Negative spot reports are equally important. First, you should try to correct the behavior by giving the individual all the help and guidance they deserve. The rest is up to them. You may need all the incidents written down as reference should you need to permanently remove this individual. When giving a negative spot report, the individual should be talked to as discretely as possible after the incident. You can use a blue card if you choose it to be formal or, if the incident is that severe, you can write a formal counseling statement on the action. Corrective counseling can take the form of "What were you thinking?," to "Let's go talk." Personnel in the tactical arena should be thick skinned and ready for direct and frank feedback. During rehearsals, this should be addressed in front of the team first to correct any misunderstandings with the team and to ensure that they understand what the problem was. You can then take the problem individual off to the side for a talking to. You have these options at your disposal for addressing the problem:

- Discuss off to the side at the individual level
- Discuss in front of the group and let it be.
- Discuss in front of the group and jot it down for future reference.
- Discuss in front of the group and give a spot report later.
- Discuss in front of the group and formally counsel.
- Discuss in front of the group and remove from training.

If you think it is just an isolated incident, you can let it be. If you are not sure if it is an isolated incident, you can jot down the incident on a blue card and keep it for record. If it is serious enough, you can give the individual a spot report and counseling of the incident, having them sign the spot report indicating they were counseled. The next level of seriousness is to give the person a formal counseling statement either the same day or the next day to ensure they know it was a serious infraction. If the infraction is a safety issue that cannot be tolerated, you can dismiss the candidate from training and have them report later for counseling or counsel immediately. The choice is yours. It is important to remember that you have many tools and levels of discretion to use when working with your people.

Achievement awards are simple tools that a leader can use to reward exceptional performance. Use them when you have a team player who exceeds the standards and consistently performs in an exceptional manner. Officers I have worked for have used the term "tools" to describe the use of awards. These pathetic officers are not real leaders. Routinely they would change the standard for receiving the award to their own personal standard and sometimes made it a personality contest or a political tool. Awards are simple. If someone takes the time to do something great, you as a leader should take the time to see that they are rewarded for their effort.

## THE IMPORTANCE OF AN OUTSIDE PERSPECTIVE

Outside perspectives can be accomplished by pulling your assistant team leader to the side and asking them their opinion on the person or incident in question. If they are too close to the problem you could ask another team leader their opinions on the matter. If you wish to involve upper leadership, you could ask your boss and get their two-cents worth, first ensuring that they will not take action without your recommendation. Most good leaders won't, but occasionally you will get one that may have a grudge against either the person or the action the person did and wants to jump the gun and hammer them instead of letting you use your tools to work it out.

I used video in training as another way to ensure that you're getting an accurate picture of what happened during the performance of team member in a particular scenario. Military and law enforcement conduct training that is more hazardous than other types, since there is zero tolerance for safety mistakes or sloppiness. You may wish to target this area because an individual is having problems with decisions or is occasionally sloppy with a muzzle. In Special Operations most students were washed out of training for either safety violations, discrimination or for close quarter battle (CQB) problems. CQB requires a constant focus on safety and discrimination. New candidates who could not execute CQB drills safely and properly discriminate or identify targets, would be terminated. Zero tolerance. In Special Operations we could not fail a mission by shooting a fellow soldier or innocent hostage. It was simply unacceptable. I remember going through training when the team was focusing on one of the members who was having a problem in CQB and we would hesitate for a moment, watching him and his muzzle out of self preservation before we would engage threat targets. It was unsettling for a week or so, but he got on board with the program and finished the training. In this case, had the instructors deemed it necessary, they could have removed him from training. The individual in question was probably being formally counseled without our knowing and had been walking a tightrope the entire time.

# ADMINISTRATIVE REQUIREMENTS

One of the biggest complaints I hear from the law enforcement community is that an individual belongs to a union or a civil service and they can't be terminated. This is a sad state that requires leadership to routinely document deficiencies and build a "packet" on the individual who is a hazard or safety problem. If you think the paperwork required is tough now, wait until you have a training accident or a problem on a raid and the investigation and law suits start. I strongly suggest that as a leader or administrator, you handle safety and discrimination problems quickly and decisively before they turn ugly and disrupt morale.

Resolution of safety problems or similar issues can take the form of formal counseling or even reassignment. The biggest problem I have witnessed is the lack of counseling and paperwork when it comes to getting rid of someone not suited for the job. Generally no one wants to hurt someone's feelings or put a black mark on their record, so they don't write anything down. They quietly slide this person to another job and things die down and people forget. Leadership will eventually change and this person will continue to compete for promotion to be a candidate for a leadership position. If an individual is in an assignment because he screwed up, resulting in a training accident, and there is no paperwork to back it up, someone did not have the nerve or professionalism to write it down. Now this individual with the problems (and has not fixed them) is promoted and in charge of more people. I have witnessed this happen too many times. I prefer to call these people "leftovers," individuals that make it through the system because they outlast the leadership rotations and most people's memories. Sadly enough in this world, you must have it documented or it does not mean squat. You can put someone away in a dark corner to work and they will not come back to bother you, but they will come back to haunt someone else. So don't harm your current or future team mates by failing to lead, counsel or take decisive action.

# TOTALITY OF AN INCIDENT

When writing a negative counseling statement, you should look at the following areas before you decide how hard to drop the hammer:
*   Severity of incident.

- Worse case potential outcome.
- Was it a training deficiency?
- Was it a failure to prepare?
- Was it a lack of attention and why?
- Attitude and demeanor of person in question before and after the incident.
- Was this an ongoing problem?

Viewing the total information available and even recreating the incident in question is not too difficult to do to reach a confident conclusion to the questions that arise over the incident. Especially in difficult or questionable investigations, it is important that you sort through all the facts to ensure your picture is accurate. The question a leader must ask themselves is "What is this person's career or life worth?" Beyond the paperwork, the leader needs to live with the decision or they will dwell on it for some time.

## TECHNIQUES AND COURSES OF ACTION

I have been fortunate to see a wide variety of counseling techniques and corrective action. The spectrum runs from verbal or monetary compensation, to removal from the organization. Much more severe techniques such as imprisonment can be seen in the regular Army.

What upsets me the most are people who waste their time and my time. As an ROTC instructor, I would bust my rear to help a cadet that wanted to help themselves. I would stay late or come in early or spend personal time if needed to get them on the right track. The ones I had no time for were the ones who would not help themselves. As they started their junior year, I would generally run three or four off out of the program the first month. I could generally tell who was serious and not serious and gave them a chance to prove it. If they did not take the opportunity I pushed them out of the program. Why? Because it was more efficient to do it now rather than to deal with them for months, writing counseling statements and babysitting them, knowing full well that I would have to fire them down the road. This way, I could concentrate on the cadets who wanted to be there; to give them my full and undivided attention. I even had kids that pulled out late in their third year, claiming that their father was a Full Bird Colonel and the only reason they stayed this long was because of him. I was happy that they found their inner strength, grew up and started making their own choices in life. They will be much happier human beings for it and the service will be much better off. The commander supported me on my appraisals 90 percent of the time and that was fine with me. The more cadets I was allowed to cull earlier in the program, the less time I would have to spend later counseling and removing them. During my time as a trainer, I kept detailed counseling statements and detailed notes on my screw-ups to save me time, work and aggravation in the long run.

Another problem with keeping poor cadets is that they could poison the well in different ways. First, they could have a bad influence on other cadets and cause morale problems. Next, other cadets would be watching you as a service member and cadre to see how you would deal with the malcontents. If you did not correct it quickly, they would assume that the service would mirror your sloppy attitude and demeanor. Most wanted a structure in their life and your inability to take control did not exude confidence in the Army. Quick and efficient removal from the program set the tone in the first month and everyone understood the rules. It made the rest of the year more pleasant.

## KEY POINTS

- COUNSEL!
- COUNSEL REGULARLY, BOTH GOOD AND BAD
- IF SOMEONE FAILS TO MAKE THE GRADE AFTER MULTIPLE COUNSELINGS, DOCUMENT AND FIRE THEM. DON'T PASS THEM ON TO OTHERS AND DON'T POISON THE WELL

# CHAPTER TWELVE

# REALITIES OF COMBAT AND TACTICAL TIPS

*"War was ugly and evil, for sure, but it was still the way things got done on most of the planet. Civilized states had nonviolent ways of resolving disputes, but that depend on the willingness on everyone involved to back down. Here in the raw Third World, people hadn't learned to back down at least not until after a lot of blood flowed. Victory was for those willing to fight and die. Intellectuals could theorize until they sucked their thumbs right off their hands, but in the real world, power still flowed from the barrel of a gun. If you wanted the starving masses in Somalia to eat, then you had to out muscle men like this Aidid, for whom starvation worked. You could send in your bleeding-heart do-gooders, you could hold hands and pray and sing hootenanny songs and invoke the great gods CNN and BBC, but the only way to finally open the roads to the big-eyed babies was to show up with more guns. And in the real world, nobody had more or better guns than America. If the good-hearted ideals of humankind were to prevail, then they needed men who could make it happen."*

Mark Bowden

- AGGRESSIVENESS-IT WILL KEEP YOU ALIVE
- SURGICAL VS. COMBAT
- INTENSITY AND REALISTIC TRAINING
- COMBAT MINDSET

## COMMAND POST

I went back out into the courtyard and found that the assault commander and several other leaders had come in off the street. My guys were still out on the street hooking and jabbing with the locals. The commander had a great deal of pressure on himself at this time and I was looking to him for some guidance, but he had too much information coming in. So much so, that he could not process it all and give directions at the same time. Present were two section sergeant majors, another captain and Pete, a team leader who had come in and backed me up when I started clearing the house. The volume of fire was picking up and it seemed that we were receiving much more than we were giving. One of the section sergeant majors told me to go check on my guys and it pissed me off. I knew my guys were okay, my ATL was with them and I had left them for an hour before on a different hit with another team leader. It was obvious that the additional leadership had nothing positive to input, but would rather sit around the assault commander waiting for any scrap of information he would put out.

We had one wounded soldier from our security force laying on the floor of the CP and guys were starting to treat him. I was pissed, so I grabbed his rifle and three of his magazines and an M67 fragmentation grenade from one of his ammo pouches and headed outside. The same section sergeant majors asked me in an excited tone "you're throwing grenades." I told him I wasn't getting paid to bring them back. I turned around and I made an immediate left hand turn and moved down the wall about fifteen feet. I stacked the magazines in the dirt next to my right knee and told my guys to get in the CP. They moved past me and I started to do some shooting. I used the wounded soldier's rifle because it would shoot as well as mine and I did not know how long we would be there. Also, I did not want to get my rifle dirty until I really had to. The M16A2 had a good feel to it with its long sight radius, so I started to clean the street to the north. The road to my front dipped down to the next intersection and then began to rise to the next cross street. I had a large leafy tree 35 yards to my left front, which blocked the enemy's view of me from a great portion of the road to the north. I started with deliberate aimed fire and began to put bullets into any location that could hide a human being. I started by putting rounds into the leafy tree to my front just to make sure that no bad guys had climbed up into it and were waiting for the right time to strike. I remember reading accounts of Japanese soldiers doing this during W.W. II and I just wanted to keep the locals honest.

Below the tree to my front were four to five soldiers who belonged to our blocking force and were gathered around a car that was parked next to the tree. A tin wall surrounded a courtyard on the left side of the tree. I did not like how close that courtyard wall was to the guys in our security position. I grabbed the M67 grenade, flipped off the safety catch, pulled the pin and threw it over the building, deep into the courtyard to keep any potential threats at bay. I waited and nothing. The son-of-a-bitch was a dud. I grabbed one of the foreign grenades that we used (it had the best fragmentation pattern of all grenades tested). I pulled the pin and gave it a heave in the same spot. A few seconds later it went off with a nice soft boom that composition B explosive makes.

I started working over the street again, engaging near targets and then moving farther down the street. I saw a tin shed next to the tree and began to engage it by putting two to three rounds through it at chest level and then working the floor over. My logic was that the high rounds would either hit them or drive them to them to the floor and the floor is where they would get hit. I then turned my attention to the street and put one to two rounds into every dark doorway or window in my field of view. About two-thirds my way up the street, I observed a wood picket fence made of three or four inch small vertical round logs or large branches. I methodically worked it over and moved to my next area of interest, which was the intersection 30 yards past it.

"Darters" would dash from one corner to the next, running like their hair was on fire. I would only be able to get three rounds off during their sprint. I would fire one on the leading edge of their body, one about eight inches to their front and another about one-and-one-half feet in front of them. I was hoping that they would run into one of the three bullets. I was not worried about killing them but rather to take a good chunk of meat out of their body and discourage them from coming any closer to the fight. It was about a two-city block shot, probably 150-200 meters and I could never tell if I hit anyone. At that range, they would make it across the street and then probably bleed out among friends. I would then start my shooting sequence of windows and doors and move back to the closest targets.

I remember looking to my right at the pathetic looking Black Hawk helicopter, laying on its side in the alley. There were about four or five security personnel around it, doing their best to pull security amid the incoming fire from the alley to my left. They had even resorted to pulling the Kevlar floor plates out of the bird and propping them up as shields in front of them in the dirt street. I thought to myself, "that is crazy." I watched as one security man on a knee, took a dead center hit on his "chicken plate" (ceramic plate in the vest that stops rifle bullets) and got knocked backwards. He was tough, he got back up in the same spot and guess what. He got hit again in the plate. He fell backward this time and "Darwin's Theory" kicked in and he scrambled for cover. He was a lucky man to take two hits on the chicken plate. If only one round would have glanced off his plate, it would have screamed through the Kevlar vest and ruined his day. You see the "plate" is the only thing that will stop rifle fire. The vest itself is good for only pistol rounds and fragmentation.

During this time, I was firing about a foot and a half over the security position to my front that were huddled around the car. They appeared to be "weapons tight," a term meaning that they were not shooting. I was pissed and was cussing, screaming and shooting, all at the same time. After I fired my third magazine, I decided to go back into the CP and get some more ammo. I re-entered the CP and as I did, some bad guy was trying to put rounds on me. I went back to the soldier on the ground who had so graciously allowed me to use his rifle and took three more of his magazines off his gear and headed for the gate. Rick said to be careful, that someone was trying to hit me, and I made a fast and hard left to my sweet spot next to the building where I was before. I began my same pattern of shooting and remember a woman running with an apron held out straight and it appeared that it was weighted and contained something important. She was going from the close intersection left side, running to the right side of the street. Well, the rules of engagement (ROE), were now a little more lenient. She was coming to a gunfight, probably bringing ammo and that was wrong. Several positions started to light her up and I screwed up and started tracking her head instead of her body and I broke the shot. I think it was a tracer and it went about an inch or so behind her head. One of the guys at the blocking position turned around and looked at me like I was crazy and I screamed "what the fuck are you looking at." There is no way he could have heard me because of the fire and all the stuff that was going on. He could probably tell from the demeanor on my face that I was not in a pleasant mood.

Looking to my right, I remember seeing a soldier in the middle of the street on a knee about five feet from a doorway. It looked like someone told him to go there and it was a stupid idea and poor position. I had a tree for concealment, but he had nothing but two-city blocks of enemy positions looking at him. I screamed and motioned to him to get out of the street and back to the doorway, but he either ignored me or was just following orders. An enemy gunner zeroed in on him and the rounds started impacting around him in the dirt until one connected. He held fast until hit and then rolled over. Shit. I glanced up and saw the guys from the CP were ready to dash out and get him. I started to lay down suppressive fire for their move and as my fire picked up they knew it was time to go. Two to three guys launched fast, grabbed him and drug him back to the CP. They began treatment and then called for an Air Force PJ who was working on others across the street at the downed bird. I saw he was going to make a dash from there to our position, so I started working over the street to the north, giving him some covering fire. He was moving as fast as his feet would carry him with all his gear. He made it safely and started to look over the new patients. Looking right, I saw another soldier came out into the street, about to the same spot where the first was hit. I thought to myself, "not again." I screamed and motioned, but he stayed and the entire episode repeated itself. This time, the guys from the other side of the street drug him back in to their building.

I glanced to my left and saw something fly over the tin fence from the courtyard I had thrown my grenades into. It left a small smoke trail and hit one of the security guy in the back, who was on the other side of the car to my front. Two of the men realized it was a grenade and scurried around the car to use it as cover. As luck would have it, it was a dud and did not go off. I looked at the tin fence a few feet to their left and started working it over with rifle fire. I would punch evenly spaced holes chest high across it and then work it over with a few rounds at ground level. It was starting to worry me that we were not putting enough fire out and the bad guys were getting ballsy and moving to within hand grenade range. It was starting to suck.

To add to my already fine day, the rifle that I was using jammed up at about magazine number five to six and started to double feed. This pissed me off and I moved back into the CP. As I did the enemy gunner who was tracking me, could see me as I headed in, dumped a couple of rounds off to my left into the dirt, trying to keep me honest. I told Rick as I came in, I said "I think your right, he is trying to hit me." This time I grabbed another fragmentation grenade and a LAW (Light Anti-Tank Weapon) and headed back outside. I was able to get safely into my position for a third time. I saw one of the guys from the position to my front looking down the alley to my left. I threw the LAW underhanded end over end in the air and it landed on his left arm and he jumped. I threw the frag to them also and said, "shoot the mother-fucker (LAW) and throw the fucking grenade."

It was time to start getting my issued rifle dirty as I had cleared the jammed rifle and left it in the CP. I started to shoot and work over the street again, when I saw a gunman with an AK poke his head and barrel around the corner of the right corner of the intersection to our right front. The individuals in the blocking position to the front by the car fired a few rounds, but most impacted the side of the building and glanced off. I had two more grenades left and it was the perfect time to use one. I pulled the pin and launched it over the security position and just past the corner where the gunman poked out into the center of the street. It went off and I am sure it cleaned out anyone hiding around the corner. No one else poked out of that position again.

By this time, the Air Force PJ was running low on medical supplies and needed to make a dash to the crashed bird and bring some more supplies back. He was the man. As I started to shoot, he dashed back to the bird, scrounged around for a few seconds, filled his hands with what he needed and then ran back again at break neck speed. He did a helluva of job. I pulled off my position and re-entered the CP and held by the front gate, using it as cover. I started to think my luck was beginning to run out hiding behind the visual barrier of the tree and one of these times someone may decide to shoot through the tree and get a piece of me. I tucked back in the gate and started to send a few rounds down range using the doorway as cover. My buddy started to help me out by shooting a foot over my head and about a foot back. His muzzle blast about snapped my neck and I thought I was hit with an RPG. I turned around and he was laughing. I told him to get his ass over the top of me if he wanted to shoot.

Wanting to see what progress the force was making, I left Rick at the gate and moved to the Assault Commander. He was in information overload as his "command cell" was gathered around, doing nothing but stealing oxygen. I started to look around in the courtyard and found something that I did not like. There was a building attached to the courtyard, a two-story that overlooked the courtyard that had not been cleared. It would have been easy for the bad guys to get in there and simply drop grenades into the CP. Life would suck if that happened.

Seeing this, I tried to give the Assault Commander three simple points to improve our position. The first was to tie in all the elements before it got dark and to establish fields of interlocking fire. Next was to clear the two story building and make sure the bad guys were not there or to let them occupy it. Finally, I wanted to take my team across the alley to the building by the car/tree and establish a security position there. I wanted to be able to push our perimeter out further and make the bad guys cross a great deal of open area to get to us. This would make it easier for us to see them, engage them or direct fire support on them. He said no, I that I needed to go across the street toward the crashed bird and link-up with the Combat Search and Rescue (CSAR) element. I told him that it would be better for me to push out the other way because of the fields of fire. We went back and forth a couple of times and I said, "fuck it, you're in charge." I gathered my team and held by the front door. I told them the plan and we could see two doors directly across the street from us. The left was open and occupied by friendly forces. The right was closed and this was the one I was worried about. I did not know if any bad guys were trapped in there and I wanted to clear it first. I held the team inside the gate until the sun started to set and it got dark. Once it got dark enough so that it was difficult to see the next intersection, I knew the bad guys would have a hard time seeing us. I gave the signal and waited for the squeeze. I led out and hit the door, clearing the small room first and then a second room. A barred window connected our team to the team I had seen in left doorway. It looked like this would be home for the night.....

## AFTER ACTION COMMENTS

### Sustain:

- Keep up aggressive action and momentum.
- Use accurate semi-automatic fire to suppress the enemy.

### Improve:

- Ensure soldiers use cover at all times and leaders understand what cover is when putting soldiers into position.
- Rehearse hasty defense actions dry fire and live fire, to include call for fire missions.

## AGGRESSIVENESS-IT WILL KEEP YOU ALIVE

"Wade through the wounded and vault over the dead"

I took this old saying from a dear friend, Master Chief Hershel Davis, an "old frogman," as he puts it. It is fitting and sums up the mental and physical attitude that you must strive to attain when preparing for combat operations. It is not enough that a soldier go to war. They must go with a positive and aggressive mindset that ensures when you are shot at, that you're going to hit back hard, wade through the enemy and look for more on the other side. Plan on doing this time and time again.

# SURGICAL VS. COMBAT

Everyone has a different concept of when to change from surgical to combat. The rookie police officer or new soldier on the ground will have a different perception than that of the veteran sergeant. If the sergeant or junior leader has seen their share of action, their tolerance for allowing their soldiers to get hurt will be less than an inexperienced leader. I have no time for a leader who would put their soldiers at a disadvantage over rules of engagement or that puts soldier's lives in jeopardy to comply with political directives. I have seen this happen too many times in life and have seen the "gray" area where the U. S. State Department comes in and tries to dictate ROE (Rules of Engagement) for troops in the negotiating phase of an operation. You have to make the peace before you keep the peace and the safest way to keep the peace is to control with a heavy hand until you leave.

Too often we want to release our grip and drop our security in a country and this is when we get hit. This routinely happens when operations go from Department of Defense (DOD) to Department of State (DOS). I never thought I would see Americans killed, drug and mutilated in the streets of a foreign nation, twice in ten years. First it was in Somalia and we made the mistake of doing nothing. It has happened again in Iraq and our leaders were too weak to take action again. They would rather sacrifice the few than to make "political or military waves." Part of the problem is the Clinton era military leadership that the country has inherited. This leadership knows more about politics and little of real leadership and less about honor. To allow this to happen again, without an immediate and devastating response is criminal.

Leaders should know which troops are able to perform surgical missions and which are "combat troops." Average troops without any depth of training will have a difficult time performing surgical missions and are more likely to incur more casualties when attempting such actions. They should be used for what they do best, combat actions where they can employ the force that needs to accomplish the job. The old philosophy of when someone shoots at you with a rifle, you shoot back with a machine gun or an anti-tank rocket applies here. If they shoot at you with a machine gun, you shoot back with a tank cannon. Basically, you double the force needed and you will do well in tactical encounters. Yes, you will probably inflict a few more non-combatant casualties, but they should not be keeping bad company.

If you need surgical work performed, call a surgeon or Special Operations soldiers and let them do the job. They have the time, the training budgets and are specially selected personnel to accomplish the mission with minimal casualties. Allowing them to do the job they rehearse and train for and prevent casualties

## INTENSITY AND REALISTIC TRAINING

Once you master the basics, it is important to begin to reinforce the training with simple and realistic scenarios. The visualization phase of training needs to be confirmed with mission oriented and realistic scenarios which require the individual to work with all the tools they carry on a mission. This training ensures that individual carries the proper gear and in the spot they can most efficiently use it.

I had the pleasure to meet and befriend a retired LTC who started the first ROTC program at the school where I served. He was a Korean and Vietnam veteran and all around great guy. During one exercise where cadets were going to assault a mock target, he got some old uniforms from the supply sergeant and drove around the county looking for fresh road kills. Yes, he took all the dead critters he could find and stuffed them into the uniforms and had them littered around the target for the cadets to find. Cadets were required to search the dead bodies and find intelligence papers that were planted in the remains. Some will see this as sick, but I see it as creative. Soldiers on today's battlefield will see much worst. Shredded bodies will be common on the battlefield. Simply carrying a couple of sets of rubber hospital gloves for such cases will keep the goo off your hands. One of the best books I have every read that illustrates the horrors of war were contained in E.B. Sledges "With the Old Breed." His accounts of WWII battle in the South Pacific set the standard as to the horrors of combat. Incredible stuff.

## COMBAT MINDSET

There are no guarantees in combat. I watched a highly trained Special Operations soldier take a ricochet off a wall into his forehead from an untrained soldier carrying an unzeroed AK-47, several blocks away. All I can say was that it was his time to go. Occasionally, if the bad guys sling enough lead, you will get hit if you try to move through it. Be smart, go around it when you can and stay focused. Prepare the best way you can, and give it your best shot. Trust your instincts. There are not guarantees in life, but train in a system that will give you the best chances of survival and then allow your controlled and aggressive combat mindset to do the rest. Once you come back, honestly evaluate what and how you did and implement changes to make it better.

## KEY POINTS

- BE AGGRESSIVE
- ALWAYS STAY IN THE FIGHT AND NEVER GIVE UP
- ALWAYS LOOK TO BETTER YOUR POSITION

Printed in the United States
133612LV00003B/1/A

9 781420 889505